Martin Hall's
Breaking Out To A Better Game

PGA TOUR PARTNERS CLUB

GAME IMPROVEMENT LIBRARY™

CREDITS

MARTIN HALL'S
BREAKING OUT
TO A BETTER GAME

Printed in 2007.

Tom Carpenter
Creative Director

Jen Weaverling
Production Editor

Kate Opseth
Book Design & Production

Steve Hosid
Instruction Editor/Photographer

Steve Ellis
Content Editor

Ward Clayton
Lance Stover
PGA TOUR

Special thanks to: Mike Billstein, Terry Casey, Janice Cauley, Julie Cisler and Heather Koshiol.

Acknowledgements
"To the members of the PGA TOUR Partners Club I meet at tournaments around the country: Your questions, comments and support help create articles and books that truly reflect the needs of our outstanding membership."
—*Steve Hosid*

1 2 3 4 5 6 7 8 9 10 / 10 09 08 07
© 2007 PGA TOUR Partners Club
ISBN 13: 978-1-58159-295-5

PGA TOUR Partners Club
12301 Whitewater Drive
Minnetonka, Minnesota 55343
www.partnersclubonline.com

ABOUT THE AUTHORS

Steve Hosid (left) and Martin Hall emphasize how understanding what the face of your club is doing will improve your game.

Martin Hall

Martin Hall has long been considered one of golf's top instructors and can be seen frequently on The Golf Channel's *Academy Live*. Martin also appears in the PGA TOUR Partners Club Instruction videos and in the Club's Game Improvement books. Martin is Director of Golf Instruction at Ibis Golf and Country Club located in West Palm Beach, Florida. He can be reached at 561-624-8922.

Steve Hosid

Steve Hosid is the writer and photographer for *Breaking Out*. He is the Instruction editor for *PGA TOUR Partners Magazine* and has written 16 books on golf, fitness and tennis. Steve is a member of his friend Arnold Palmer's Bay Hill Club in Orlando Florida.

CONTENTS

INTRODUCTION

Few sports can trace their origins back several centuries while enjoying the potential for tremendous future growth. Today the young and exciting players on The PGA TOUR serve as a catalyst for young golfers to take up this lifelong sport and then hone their competitive skills through competitive junior programs. Golf provides an endless world of enjoyment, at least in the beginning.

Enjoyment is what this book is about, because all too often golf becomes frustrating when you can't find improvement. Long-time players sometimes find themselves stuck in a rut and for whatever reason can't improve, can't lower their handicaps and just can't enjoy golf as much as they once did.

Golf is not a sport of instant gratification. Magic wands waved over the head of a player stuck at a 14 handicap will have no effect. You can't will yourself to a better game. But worry not! All is not lost, and a light is shining at the end of the tunnel.

Enjoyment is about to return as you "break out" of the limitations that have held your game back. Your improvement will be immediate and long lasting, and you will find the insights, techniques, tactics and drills you need all right here in *Breaking Out.*

Let's start with equipment. You can't purchase an improved game at a

house sale or buy discount clubs from a barrel. On the other hand, you won't find any improvement just by spending your hard earned dollars on the latest and greatest equipment unless it specifically fits what you need to accomplish in your game.

We'll cover a lot of ground here, much of it with help from TaylorMade, which provided an incredible amount of information, graphics and access for this book to help you learn about the golf swing and equipment just like a pro. The MATT system photos you'll find here are actually some of the best players in the world in computerized form. TaylorMade's philosophy includes using science and engineering to help all golfers, regardless of their current skill level, improve the game they currently have without having to change it at all.

But most of us really want to improve our technique. Martin Hall has long been considered one of the world's best golf instructors. Here he provides brand new and exciting instructional insight and drills to work on the part of the game that is responsible for holding most people back from improving. In Chapters 2 through 15, Martin will transform your game by working on the role of your wrists and arms during the swing. Wrist hinge takes on a practical and more helpful meaning and will have you playing better.

Pros hit the ball farther then amateurs for a number of reasons, but the most significant reason is the effective loft of their club face compared to yours at impact. Their clubface has less loft then normal at impact while yours has more loft then normal because of what your wrists and arms are doing.

Martin is the golf world's "King" in developing drills to improve players' games. The real key is getting positive or negative feedback. Practicing without any feedback is just getting exercise. You need to know what's wrong—and then feel it getting right—in order to improve.

Occasionally your body holds back improvement in your game. Gina Piazza of GMP Fitness has received the PGA TOUR Partners Club Member Approval Seal for her golf programs. The star of many stretching and golf flexibility and conditioning videos, Gina uses PGA TOUR Partners Club member Lou Rinaldi to show how to work on balance and other aspects to help your game.

This book is jam-packed with loads of golf information, most of it in picture form. You can start improving your game immediately. Right here, you have the tools that will guide you to a better game. Absorb those ideas, practice with feedback, and have fun *Breaking Out* to lower scores and more enjoyment... *A Better Game.*

—*Steve Hosid*

Martin Hall   Steve Hosid

1

A Pro's Look at the Swing

PGA TOUR players—like Fred Funk in the computerized photo at left—are the best golfers in the world. Their skill amazes galleries, millions of fans watching at home on television, those listening to the PGA TOUR Network on XM Satellite Radio, and those following the action on their computers with TOURCast.

Just like all skilled professional athletes, PGA TOUR players have the most high-tech equipment available. They have a virtual army of technicians working on their clubs each week. They are constantly trying out new equipment, and, before a club becomes a "gamer," it has been thoroughly tested and tweaked. Their equipment is a perfect match for their individual game.

These professional players possess a very high skill level, developed from hours of hard work honing their swings to perform under the pressure of competition. They have mastered the understanding of the golf swing to where they do not think about certain aspects of the game. It is that ingrained in their subconscious.

PGA TOUR players have another thing in common: their physical conditioning. That conditioning isn't measured by how much weight they can bench press or how far they can run. Their conditioning is focused on rotational flexibility, which allows them to set their bodies in the correct angles to make proficient golf swings on plane: smooth, accelerating swings that do not leak any energy along the way.

We can't all play at a PGA TOUR skill level, but that doesn't mean golfers, regardless of their present skills, can't make great strides in improvement. Golf is an imperfect game. Even the world's best players don't get it right all the time.

So how can a golfer without the available time to devote toward working on his or her game expect to improve? This book can make a difference and get you out of the rut of your current game. TOUR Players will show you swing positions not generally covered in golf magazines, books or instruction videos. You will discover what the pros do in their swings that average golfers never know or simply misunderstand.

In this book, thanks to the cooperation and graciousness of TaylorMade Golf, you will learn about advances in equipment that can help your game without changing your swing. You will also see key swing positions of PGA TOUR players, thanks to TaylorMade's proprietary computerized swing analysis program, the MATT system.

INSTRUCTION

With all the fantastic equipment out there, who needs to take lessons to improve? Virtually everyone, including the pros. Some of today's golf instructors are just as well known as the players they work with.

This book is privileged to feature Martin Hall, who not only knows the game but also is one of golf instruction's finest communicators. He relates to his students and makes learning fun.

EVALUATING YOUR GAME

How well do you know your game? You may be a 12 handicap or a 20 or a 6, but what is your individual handicap for various phases of your game? For example, what is your handicap as a putter, off the tee, from 150 yards out?

As part of the first step toward improvement, carry a diary in your bag and keep track of fairways hit, greens in regulation, sand saves and putts per round. In other words, start breaking your game down into categories within the overall game.

VIDEOTAPE YOUR SWING

Video is one of the finest teaching aids available. A teacher can tell you what you are doing right or wrong, but until you actually see yourself in action, the message doesn't have the same impact. If you tape your swing, are you really seeing what you are doing? Not if you set the camera up at the wrong angle to view it.

WRONG FOR DOWN THE LINE

You will be scratching your head, just like Martin Hall, trying to understand what you are seeing if you place the camera on the target line when shooting from behind and toward the target. From this view, your swing will look more inside to out than it really is.

VIEW THE SWING PLANE CORRECTLY

Videotaping from behind and toward the target allows you to see your swing plane if you set the camera precisely in the right spot.

•Aim the camera right at the edge of the swing plane.

•Start up close to your position and then bring it back.

•Place the camera a good 2 ½ feet inside the target line.

•Position the camera waist high.

•If the ball is not in the bottom right quadrant of the television screen, the camera angle is not very good.

FACE ON

When the camera is placed to shoot directly at you from the front, it is called face on. This view has only one correct position.

•Mark a target line with a ball.

•Place a shaft in the ground behind the ball.

•Place another shaft starting at the ball and extending away at 90 degrees.

•You don't see the second shaft because the vertical shaft hides it.

•This is the correct camera position.

INCORRECT FACE-ON VIEWS

These two camera positions reveal the 90-degree shaft, so they are wrong. Only when you don't see the second shaft do you know the camera is positioned correctly.

SELF-EVALUATE YOUR GAME

Everyone gets lucky and hits shots they remember for the rest of their lives. Unless that is a typical shot, the memories are just that … memories. They certainly are not an indication of the quality of your game. In fact, a false idea of where your game really stands may be holding back your progress.

Evaluating your game by hitting a number of shots from the same location and then evaluating where they finished relative to your intended target is a good self-test. How many should you hit? There is no set rule, but five balls from each location would be a fair number to give you a handle on your game.

The real answer to breaking out is the area this book really gets into: what the wrists and arms do through the hitting area. These actions pertain to all facets of the game. That begins in Chapter 2. Before you begin, take some time to give your game some self-evaluation.

Demonstrating a way to test your short-game skills are two PGA TOUR Partners Club members from New York, Lou Rinaldi and his son Mike. Lou is a world-class athlete who played professional soccer and now runs a very successful construction business. Mike travels the world as an executive for IBM.

Evaluating your game is a good way to start down the road to breaking out of the rut your game may be in.

MIKE AND LOU RINALDI

Lou is a member of one of the most beautiful country clubs in the world, Trump National in Briarcliff Manor, New York. Donald Trump made sure that this club is spectacular. The course is magnificent and a very difficult test of golf. Lou is a former club champion—although he did lose the next year to Donald, who is an excellent golfer himself. You will learn more about Lou's training aid, THE GROOVE, later in the book. It took Lou from a high double-digit handicapper to scratch. In this section he helps son Mike evaluate his short game.

Mike started with short, then long putts, and then chips and pitches. The results gave Mike a clear picture of the current state of his short game.

FIVE-FOOT PUTTS

On Trump National Club's famed par-3 waterfall hole, Mike is holing one from five feet. That's good, but his shot pattern shows some distance control problems on the downhill side. Look at the pattern, not just one ball.

CHIPPING

Lou watches as Mike chips five balls uphill. Not a bad shot pattern. Mike's preference is to use a more-lofted club and have little roll after landing. A teaching pro might suggest another way to chip with a less-lofted club and more roll once it clears the fringe.

From some significant rough that is water-soaked, Mike pitches two balls within a three-foot circle, one ball within seven feet and two balls rolled off the green. What does that say about his pitching from long, wet grass? He would have had: two pars, one par or bogey (the seven-foot shot) and two potential double bogeys.

LEFT HAND CHECK

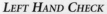

Mike and Lou evaluate the results of the test. Mike's short game is indicative of someone who really does not have the time to practice as much as he would like. He could sharpen up the results. Looking at his short swings also reveals that he can profit from the rest of this book, which reveals the pros' secret positions and how to make them part of your game.

MATT TO THE RESCUE

PGA TOUR Partners Club member Russ Post loves golf. He plays whenever his family and business responsibilities allow. His lessons several years ago with teacher and friend Jimmy Ballard brought his handicap down to a single digit, but he continued playing with his old clubs.

Russ was the perfect candidate for a cutting-edge swing analysis combined with replacing his old equipment with a set of clubs custom built to optimize his game. TaylorMade adopted Russ as a "virtual" member of its TOUR Staff for a day and gave him a new set of clubs and TaylorMade TOUR Staff Bag.

How the MATT System Works

TaylorMade developed MATT—Motion Analysis Technology by TaylorMade—to provide the most accurate method of swing analyses as a basis for performance-enhancing clubfitting. Once the computer programming inputs the swing, MATT determines the exact club specifications to optimize the tested golfer's game.

COMPUTERIZED IMAGE

MATT transposes golfers to the computer via a special outfit similar to the one Tiger Woods uses for his video game. The computer's multiple cameras pick up the sensors positioned on the hat, vest, waist, knees, shoes, special club and ball to convert Russ to the computer image.

THE PROCESS

Russ swings, and the cameras and computer analyze and measure all body positions from setup to finish, swing speed, swing plane, clubhead position at impact, launch angle, ball speed, carry and shot shape.

THE COMPUTERIZED RESULTS

Although primarily a club-fitting tool, the MATT system is also an incredible teaching system because the swing can be stopped at any point for analysis. The image can be rotated 360 degrees, and lines can be drawn in to measure and evaluate certain points or flaws.

TaylorMade staff players like Tom Lehman, Sergio Garcia, Mike Weir, Fred Funk and Darren Clarke regularly visit The Kingdom, the building at TaylorMade headquarters in Carlsbad, California, where MATT is housed, to undergo the same session Russ was privileged to experience. Swings from the past can be placed next to a player's current swing to evaluate differences.

Throughout this book you will see MATT System computer photos of TOUR players' swing positions. They are used to help illustrate what instructor Martin Hall is teaching you with his drills.

Before moving on, look at how the swing of our fellow Club member, Russ Post, a low handicap amateur, compares with the swing of PGA TOUR star Sergio Garcia.

INCORRECT HIP TILT

In the pre-test interview, Russ revealed that he had been losing distance and accuracy leading up to the clubfitting. His setup position shows the reason: A sore back, which he suffered weeks earlier, inadvertently caused Russ' right hip to be significantly higher than his left at address. This had infiltrated his setup, even after his back felt better. MATT allows the analyst to place key lines on the screen to dramatically show actual body-part-to-golf-swing relationships.

LIMITED SHOULDER ROTATION

The raised right hip restricted Russ' shoulder rotation, contributing to his loss of distance. You can learn from this how important it is to verify and work on your setup position on a regular basis, even in front of a mirror at home. In this case the hips acted as a swing-speed inhibitor by not being level.

SERGIO-RUSS COMPARISON

The MATT System contains a library of golf swings from current and former TaylorMade TOUR Staff players. Russ (silver) was compared with Sergio Garcia (red). Even with the difference in their ages, Russ' restricted shoulder turn could be traced to his hip position.

Notice the difference in shoulder and clubhead positions between Sergio and Russ. Notice that while Sergio's left elbow rotates back inside his right foot, Russ' left arm barely rotates to his right knee. On the downswing, with less distance to rotate toward the ball, Russ' clubhead speed is limited.

COMPUTER IMPACT

With this view from the ground up, notice how Russ' clubface is slightly closed at impact. The data in the previous photo registered it as -6.0° closed. Clubfitting—with proper shaft selection—will correct some ball flight flaws.

THE STATS

TaylorMade's MATT System printed out the following numbers, comparing the swings of Sergio and Russ. Both were hitting drivers.

BOX	RUSS	SERGIO
Clubhead speed at impact	94.7 mph	117.4 mph
Ball speed at launch	133 mph	167 mph
Launch angle	10.4	10.6
Backspin	2473 rpm	3835 rpm
Swing through impact zone	level	low to high
Carry	176.6 yards	266.1 yards
Face heading	-6.0 degrees closed	+3.4 degrees open

EQUIPMENT

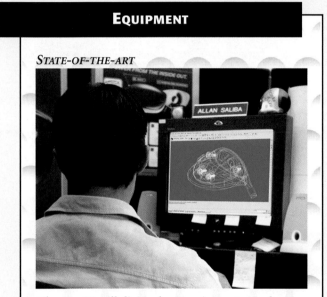

STATE-OF-THE-ART

ALLAN SALIBA

Chapter 16 will discuss how equipment can play an important role in improving your game. Clubfitting has become very sophisticated. Launch monitors have helped manufacturers custom fit their players based on the computer's definition of optimum launch angles and hang time, and are now being used to fit amateurs. Shafts are custom selected for their kick points and other characteristics best suited to the individual being fitted.

Today's golf ball technology is very sophisticated and can be matched to an individual player's game. Low spin and higher launch angles are the buzzwords in custom fitting. Golf club design is also enhanced by computers. The monitor (above) shows the weighting of a new driver.

BREAKING OUT
WORK LIST FOR SUCCESS

1. Start with an honest evaluation of where your game is now.

2. On a scorecard or in a small diary keep track of your fairways hit, greens in regulation, sand saves and putts per round.

3. If you don't have a video camera, spend some time in front of your mirror looking at positions in your swing—address, ball position, posture, grip. Don't correct; just look at them so you have an idea how you compare to the pros when you reach that chapter.

4. If you have a chance, visit the library or go online to look at some of the swings of pros like Jack Nicklaus and Ben Hogan. Look especially at their arm and wrist positions in the hitting zone.

5. Most of all, be very optimistic. One of golf's greatest teachers of this era is about to help you change your game, get you out of a rut and help you learn what the pros do that now you will be able to do, too!

WHAT THE PROS KNOW AND YOU DON'T

When I say my students improve, that doesn't mean they all improve all the time. When they don't, I try to figure out why. What is it that they don't understand?

I ask if they are practicing. If they say yes, that prompts a deeper, more relevant question: "How do you practice?" More often than not they will say: "I go to the range and beat balls!"

If that is your response, then, honestly, you are not practicing. You are exercising. The negative effect of practicing in that way makes incorrect techniques more permanent and more difficult to correct.

Almost every student I've taught has improved when he or she practices with accurate feedback. If you make an error, then someone or something has to tell you that it was an error. Once you know what caused it, then you can take the correct steps to improve. But if the ball is your only source of feedback, you will find the road to improvement extremely difficult and frustrating.

Here is a statement that you could never have pried out of me 20 years ago: "I think you can improve by hitting balls into a net in your backyard." That doesn't mean you can learn everything there is about golf by hitting into the net, but you can learn a lot. Of course, there is one important improvement ingredient that must be added to that statement: "You must have accurate feedback on what you are doing." Hitting into a backyard net without accurate feedback would be wasting your time.

If your current actions are not producing the results you want, you need to change the motion. Golf improvement is about changing the motion. When you watch great players like Tiger Woods, Vijay Singh and Tom Lehman, what is so tremendous is the dynamics of their motion.

The dynamics of the motion—how energy is thrown out to the head of the club on the downswing—is overlooked in teaching. Instead, the emphasis is put on the statics. Static golf, for example, deals with grip, posture and where the shaft is at the top of the backswing, to list a few elements. The dynamics of the swing are more important than the positions.

Unless you freeze the action, it is difficult to analyze swing motion. I like to refer to the illusionist factor. A magician is really an illusionist. What you think you see is not what is really going on. The real, but hidden, truth is that you create angles in the backswing to create velocity. The better the player you are, the more correctly those angles straighten out.

Simply, you start with a shaft and left arm that are in a line at address, and then have to take them out of line during the backswing. The level of your skill as a player is determined by how and when you get the shaft and left arm in a line again. When does that occur in your downswing?

This rarely discussed aspect in the golf swing is the single most relevant factor regarding what may be holding back your progress and what is leading to the frustration of staying in a performance rut.

WHAT MADE SERGIO GARCIA A BETTER PLAYER?

By working on his swing dynamics, Sergio Garcia has improved his ball striking. As you look at three photos that show his old swing (red) and his new swing (silver), which of the three photos illustrates the most important factor in Sergio's improvement?

BACKSWING PHOTO

TRANSITION PHOTO

While all three images are interesting and show progress, the past-impact photo is the most important photo.

Sergio's improvement can best be understood by looking at his silver swing version and noticing the straight line that extends down from his left arm through the shaft of the club. This straight line is the "secret of the pros." They know about it, and now you do, too!

PAST-IMPACT PHOTO

Bubba at Impact

Lefty Bubba Watson is the longest driver on the PGA TOUR, averaging over 320 yards in one recent year. In his case, his skill level can be seen by the straight line formed through his left arm and golf shaft just past impact.

Breaking Out
Work List for Success

1. In the next chapter, you'll learn why your wrist positions help achieve the dynamic swing motion, just like the pros'.

2. Start practicing to receive feedback on what you are doing.

3. Videotape your golf swing and freeze the action just past impact.

4. Develop a teacher's eye and concentrate on the line of the left arm and shaft just past impact. Are they in line?

IT'S ALL IN THE WRISTS

If you are a right-handed golfer, you want the shaft and your left arm to work together as if they were connected by a steel rod. The rod must remain stiff before the hitting area and to a point well after impact. Left-handers should have that same feeling, but for them it is the shaft and right arm. Throughout this book, we will primarily use the right-handed player for demonstration purposes.

Feeling this "steel rod" connection helps you better understand that the left wrist does not flap or bend through this extremely important phase of the swing. Not bending the left wrist is the idea to hold firmly in your mind. However, left wrist cock, as you'll see, is okay. Just before, during and after impact, having this "steel rod" look is what separates the better players from those who struggle. Another way to phrase this is: A "steel rod" look connecting your left arm and the shaft separates those who *can* from those who cannot.

THE STEEL ROD CONNECTION

Wearing the steel rod connection device that begins this chapter, the following photo sequence provides the correct left wrist and shaft position needed to develop real improvement. Honestly, there is no other position in golf as important as this. For emphasis, I'm demonstrating with just my left arm.

ENTERING IMPACT AREA

PRE-IMPACT

AFTER IMPACT

Notice a bit of wrist cock at this position, as the club comes down the swing plane into the impact area.

There is still some wrist cock just before impact. Also, notice my left hand is ahead of the clubface. This is another difference between good and poor players and one of the reasons pros hit farther than most recreational golfers.

See the straight line between my left arm and the shaft: the real power position that pros understand but most golfers do not.

ADDRESS AND IMPACT ARE NOT ALIKE

One misconception that sticks in most golfers' minds is that they have to replicate the address position at impact. Nothing in golf could be farther from the truth.

ADDRESS

A good address position should look like this. Now compare this with the correct impact position.

IMPACT

Can you see the difference? My hands are ahead of the clubhead at impact.

POSITIVE RESULTS

When your hands are ahead at impact, you can achieve this powerful past-impact position. Notice the wrists have not flipped or flapped.

PROBLEM

Avoid this position if real improvement is your goal! The hands are incorrectly behind the ball at impact. The reason? The left arm does not have the steel rod relationship with the shaft. Avoid this movement at all costs.

PROBLEM RESULTS

The steel rod relationship between the left arm and shaft is clearly missing in this photo. The wrist and arm should be lined up, not breaking as seen here. Power loss! Accuracy loss! This motion keeps you in a rut and prevents improvement.

WHY UNDERSTANDING WRIST POSITIONS IS IMPORTANT

I'll demonstrate exactly what each wrist should be doing, but first, as a way to ease into further understanding and remove old myths that so many golfers have, let's discuss each wrist's distinctive motions in the swing.

WRISTS: COCKED AND UNCOCKED

Soon you will discover that only the left wrist cocks and uncocks. First to promote a better understanding of the term, I'll demonstrate this with both wrists. This refers to the wrists' vertical movement.

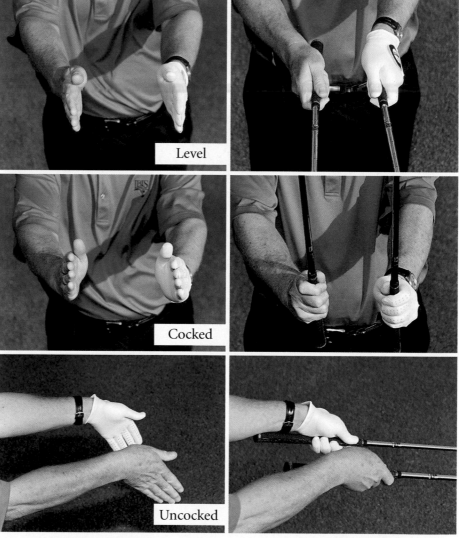

Starting from a level position (top), the wrists cock (middle) and then uncock (bottom).

CHALK TALK

SIX THINGS THE WRISTS CAN DO IN THE GOLF SWING:

1. Cock	3. Turn	5. Bend
2. Uncock	4. Roll	6. Arch

WRISTS: TURNED AND ROLLED

To understand turning and rolling, the key is to watch what happens to the clubface. Notice the position of the face as I demonstrate turning and rolling my wrists.

For demonstration only, notice that when starting from the level position, as I turn my wrists the clubface turns to a position facing up in the air. When I roll them the clubface also rolls into a position facing the ground. Later, you will learn the left hand and wrist control the clubface during the swing.

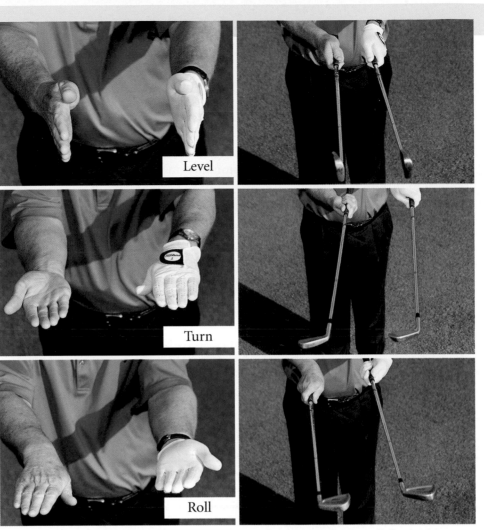

Level

Turn

Roll

Starting from a level position (top), the wrists turn (middle) and then roll (bottom).

WRISTS: BEND AND COCK

The all-important reason to understand these defining terms as to what the wrists are doing is so that when you hear "*cock your wrists*," you don't misunderstand the terminology and bend them instead. This is especially true of the term bend and cock.

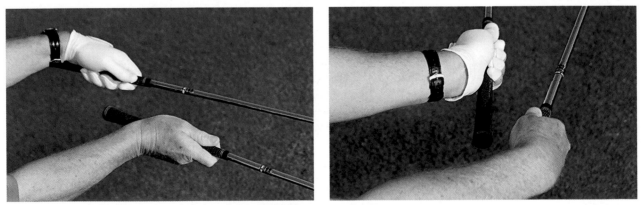

These photos incorrectly show both wrists performing the same motions. It's easy to understand why many golfers have a problem understanding the concept that each wrist has its own function during the swing rather than mimicking each other. The key to a pro's swing is to work with the idea that each wrist has a hinge on it. The left wrist hinge would be on top so the wrist can hinge only up and down but not side to side. The right wrist has a hinge on the back of the wrist allowing it only to hinge side to side but never up and down. With that in mind, can you now understand why both these photos are demonstrating incorrect mimicking motions.

OTHER TERMS TO UNDERSTAND

Improvement comes from understanding, and, like any business or hobby, golf does have its own language. Sometimes singular becomes plural by mistake (wrist cock), and sometimes a general term can also lead to misunderstanding.

Here are a few concepts it pays to understand. Often the correct interpretation differs from your current understanding as to what they mean or refer to.

FLAT LEFT WRIST AT IMPACT

Why do you need a flat left wrist during your swing? I didn't realize—as I'm sure many pros and legions of golfers down through the ages didn't realize—that just a couple degrees of bend in the left wrist is enough to ruin your game.

Because the left wrist controls the clubface, any bend misaligns the face, causes the acceleration to be erratic, and very often causes you to hit the ground before the ball. If you can think of anything evil with that clubface, the left wrist can do it if the position is not flat. Many golfers fling their wrists during the swing. It is the most natural thing to do, but it's not what good players do.

Of course, if your grip is a strong one, like that of Paul Azinger, Ed Fiore and David Duval, you won't have a flat left wrist. It is, however, their equivalent of flat, as the shaft and the left arm will still be in line.

RELEASING THE WRISTS

No picture for this one because the entire thought of releasing the wrists is wrong! Releasing the wrists is one of those concepts that is so misleading that it causes you to stay in a learning rut trying to make it happen. With today's still cameras and high-speed digital video, we can closely analyze the best golf swings of yesterday and today.

Absolutely no superior player has had his or her shaft pass the left arm either at or just after impact. Perhaps the misunderstanding comes from how pros explain what they do. Jack Nicklaus may say he releases, but he's not referring to some wristy, flappy, bending of the left wrist through the hitting area. Jack is describing how he uncocks his left wrist.

One theme you will see throughout this book is that the left wrist should cock and uncock, while the right wrist should bend and unbend. You will never read here that the wrists release, as each wrist has a very specific motion. Cocking and uncocking the left wrist produces speed. Bending the left wrist on the other hand, would be disastrous. So erase the releasing term from your mind because it only leads to bending both wrists past impact, and that, as you are learning, has been holding you back.

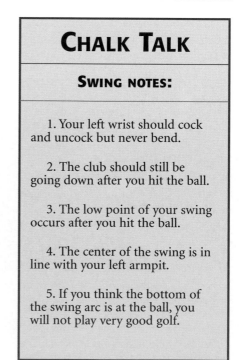

CHALK TALK

SWING NOTES:

1. Your left wrist should cock and uncock but never bend.

2. The club should still be going down after you hit the ball.

3. The low point of your swing occurs after you hit the ball.

4. The center of the swing is in line with your left armpit.

5. If you think the bottom of the swing arc is at the ball, you will not play very good golf.

Why Pros Hit It Farther

Part of the reason pros hit the ball so far is that their hands are ahead and the steel rod relationship maintains itself. Let's see if you can analyze the next two photos for the main clue why pros hit it farther.

You probably noticed the top left photo is the address position and the top right photo is the hands-ahead-at-impact position you will be working on. Earlier, we dealt with the misconception that you must return to your address position at impact; however, the next two photos (below) illustrate the top right photo creates the longer hit.

Hands Ahead = Stronger Club

Pros de-loft the club, making it stronger, with their hands are ahead of the ball at impact. Higher handicappers add additional loft to the club at impact by incorrect motion, especially the misconstrued concept of releasing their wrists. (Hopefully, you have now learned to avoid releasing like the plague.)

The difference in lofts at impact becomes very significant. Tiger Woods will frequently de-loft a club by as much as 12 degrees at impact as a result of having his hands ahead. If you add a few degrees of loft, say three degrees, by flipping through impact, you already have a 15-degree loft difference from the address position between you and Tiger.

Tiger is now playing a club that has 15 degrees less loft than the same club in your hands. That will definitely affect how far the ball goes. Clubs have two different types of loft:

•Static loft—the loft built naturally into the club.

•Dynamic loft—the only loft that counts because it occurs when you hit the ball. The ball doesn't care about anything other than the dynamic loft. It doesn't see static loft at impact.

A de-lofted club due to hands ahead at impact.

A more standard loft, due to hands aligned with impact.

Breaking Out
Work List for Success

1. Using a full-length indoor mirror, set up at your normal address position. (Note that we may change that address position later.)

2. Simulate what you have learned your swing should look like at dynamic impact. Are your hands ahead of the ball?

3. As you extend just past impact do you now have a straight line formed by your left arm and the shaft? That is the key position.

4. Notice how the clubface is de-lofted at impact with your hands ahead instead of lagging incorrectly behind.

5. Using the mirror, hold two clubs in front and repeat the six wrist positions demonstrated on pages 24 and 25.

4

POSITIVE PRACTICE:
THE PROS' DYNAMIC
POSITION DRILLS

The drills in this chapter will begin the process that will have you breaking out of the rut you may be in that is hindering improvement. Just like anything you want to succeed at, improvement takes a bit of work to master.

Positive feedback is important, and, while I may be using certain items in these drills, you can be creative and improvise by finding items around your home that offer some similarity. Don't be put off by not having the absolute items I use to demonstrate. Remember that golf is a game of adapting to the circumstances.

DRILL: THE LOWEST POINT OF YOUR SWING

The purpose of this drill is to understand that the low point of your swing is under your left armpit.

The drills beginning on the next page teach you to hit the ball on the downswing so the lowest point of your swing arc occurs after you have struck the ball. You must first strike the ball, and then let the club continue going into the ground, to program your mind that the lowest point is under your left armpit.

To be honest, you will find the first drill difficult. It significantly moves what you thought was the lowest point of your swing. In most cases, it will be slightly forward of where it may be now. Some students have said it is a very humbling drill, but my answer is that it is not humbling, it is informative.

STARTING SUGGESTIONS

Work on this drill gradually by starting with a small swing instead of a full one. It won't do you any good just to read it; you must actually *do* it if you want to break out and improve.

In a piece of plywood, make a notch wider than a clubhead and about six inches long. Place a tee level to a shaft that you've placed on the plywood about two inches from the back of the notch.

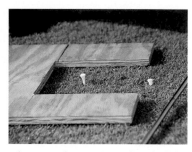

Place another tee just ahead of the notch. Make the tee level with the shaft when it rests on the ground.

Now, address the ball with the forward tee on line with your left armpit. The forward tee represents the actual lowest point in the swing arc. You want to hit this tee, not the first one.

Start slowly with a backswing that brings the club back only to a position parallel to the ground.

Swing the club back toward the tees, with the shaft tilted forward as a result of your hands being ahead of the clubhead.

With your hands still leading, swing over the first tee. Notice the left arm and the shaft have not quite reached the in-line steel rod position at this point.

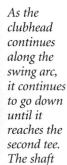

As the clubhead continues along the swing arc, it continues to go down until it reaches the second tee. The shaft position is forward tilted as a result of your hands being ahead of the clubhead. Notice how the line of the left arm and shaft straightens at this impact position.

The clubhead impacts the second tee. The forward shaft lean de-lofts the club, making it stronger, just like the pros'.

A drill that provides negative feedback is very important in the learning process. Remember our goal was only to hit the second tee.

In both Negative Feedback photos, the straight shaft at impact is incorrect and has resulted in two negative feedback situations.

In the first photo at left, the clubhead hit the plywood, indicating you made a mistake.

In the second photo at left, the clubhead was also fairly straight, and the result was hitting the higher first tee instead of swinging down over it to impact the second tee at what is really the lowest point of the swing arc.

THE 911 DRILL

This drill is potent medicine for erasing some incorrect swing thoughts that may be holding you back. You will learn to have your hands ahead into and after impact without leaving the clubface open, a common mistake I see when I advise my students to move their hands forward through the impact zone. If you think of de-lofting the club, you will automatically move your hands ahead.

This is not a motion drill, but it will program your mind to the hands-forward position. You need a 2 x 4 scrap of lumber. You can practice this drill indoors as well as outside.

STARTING POINT

Place the clubface against the lumber.

ADDRESS   *DE-LOFT THE CLUB*

Start with the clubface still pressed against the lumber. De-loft the clubface by keeping the face against the lumber as the shaft tilts forward. This drill demonstrates how the hands must be ahead of the ball without opening the face of the club.

Put yourself in a good address position.

CHALK TALK

LET THE 911 DRILL RALLY TO YOUR AID:

1. Hold the de-lofted position for five seconds.

2. Close your eyes and feel where the back of your left hand is.

3. With your eyes closed, feel where your right hand and your body are located in order for you to reach this position.

4. Feel the difference between the address and impact positions.

5. Once you have the feeling, hit a few shots with a partial swing. Try a swing that goes from 9 o'clock to 3 o'clock.

Positive
Practice:
The Pros'
Dynamic
Position
Drills

MUST-DO DRILL

Do this drill every day to break out of any current non-improving frustration. This is the ultimate drill for feeling a flat left wrist. You learn why you haven't been playing very well, and then, in a very positive manner, how to turn that around and begin to play very well.

THE EQUIPMENT

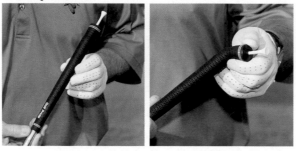

I'm using a small piece of the butt end of a shaft, and I have slipped on a grip that does not go completely to the end. Insert a tee in the end of the grip.

RIGHT-HAND GRIP

Position the right hand on the club as you would normally, except lower down the shaft.

LEAD

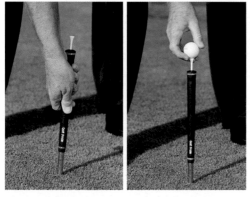

Place the shaft in the ground and a ball on the tee. This provides the feeling of a very high tee.

LEFT-HAND GRIP

The key is to grip down onto the shaft with the left hand. Place the shaft along the palm of the left hand much more than I would normally recommend. If done correctly, you should have the grip touching the inside of your left forearm.

BALL BACK IN STANCE   ### SWING

The correct normal ball position should be under your left armpit. For this drill, you do need to position the ball slightly back in your stance.

Very slowly swing the club back slightly and then through the ball, knocking it off the tee. The shaft must always be in contact with the arm throughout this swing. Notice how the left arm and shaft are lined up through the swing.

CHALK TALK

Q: WHERE IS THE LOW POINT OF THE SWING?

A: THE TARGET SIDE OF THE BALL.

The low point of the swing is not when you hit the ball. It is past impact on the target side of the ball. It is on the other side that faces your target. This is why the club still swings downward following impact.

LOWEST POINT DRILL

A weighted string easily demonstrates where the lowest point of the swing really is.

To demonstrate that the lowest point of my swing is not in line with my head but the armpit of my left shoulder, I've put a tee in the ground on line with my head and tied a weight to the end of the string.

Hold the string by the top and by your left armpit. Allow the string to move in a pendulum motion. It becomes perpendicular to the ground not at the tee but at your left armpit. Notice that the string, like a shaft, is tilted forward as it descends.

LOWEST POINT DRILL #2

Using the tee on top of the grip from the Must-Do Drill, I'll demonstrate the bottom of the swing arc again, this time with a swinging club.

In this example I've teed the ball just to the right of my left armpit. I bring the club back to create the momentum that will swing it through the ball.

Notice how the club becomes vertical, the lowest part of the swing, after impacting the ball.

CHALK TALK

WHAT HAVE WE LEARNED?

Except for the driver and the putter, always position the ball slightly to the right of the low point. Simply put, this should be about a ball's width back to the right side. This is how the low point becomes the target side of the ball instead of at the ball.

THE IMAGE DRILL

A MORE REALISTIC 'TAP' DRILL

Sometimes I like to take examples to the extreme. Golf is a game full of enjoyment, and even though some of my examples are a little exaggerated, they are the ones you will remember as mental images. You need a good mental image to help you break out of not improving. Once you understand and then can adapt your game to what you're seeing and reading here, then improvement will become obvious. Purpose: To create the mental image of hitting a nail into the ground with a hammer.

MENTAL IMAGE 1

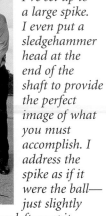

I've set up to a large spike. I even put a sledgehammer head at the end of the shaft to provide the perfect image of what you must accomplish. I address the spike as if it were the ball—just slightly back of my left armpit.

MENTAL IMAGE 2

I've swung the hammer shaft back to about waist high. As I start the forward swing, my hands will lead all the way. This drill specifically demonstrates that you will drive a nail into the ground with more power if your hands are ahead at impact rather than incorrectly trailing.

MENTAL IMAGE 3

Power, Power, Power! Notice my hands are ahead of the hammer's head. No energy has been used up early by incorrectly flipping the wrists.

MENTAL IMAGE 4

Impact position. The hands-ahead position brings the hammer's head to the spike with a powerful descending blow. Notice how the hammer's head matches up to the spike's angle.

Now it is your turn. This drill accomplishes exactly what the last one did, but it is easily done with items in your golf bag: a club and a tee.

Your goal is to tap a tee into the ground with your club in a hands-ahead, forward-tilted shaft position. Drills like these are good reminders during a round or on the range between shots. They provide positive feedback and keep your mind programmed correctly.

SET THE TEE

Begin by inserting a golf tee partially into the ground at an angle.

BACKSWING

A powerful downswing is not needed to tap the tee into the ground, so take the club only slightly back.

TAP THE TEE

With the hands ahead, which tilts the shaft forward, just bring the club back to the tee softly enough to tap it. At this point you should start feeling the hands-forward position as normal.

THE SHOVE DRILL

Two pieces of lumber will provide positive practice feedback if you do this drill correctly and shove lumber pieces together. If you don't, the drill will provide equally important negative feedback. Either way, your practice becomes very worthwhile. This drill will get you away from scooping, and from bending your left wrist. An added benefit is that doing hand drills makes you aware that less-proficient golfers hit with too much force from their hands.

PREPARE

Cut a four-inch piece of wood off the end of a 2 x 4. Place both pieces about three inches apart.

BACKSWING

After swinging slightly back from the wood, bring the club back down to the wood with the hands ahead.

CORRECT IMPACT

Shove the two pieces of wood together. Notice how the club is de-lofted as in the earlier drill we did with a static piece of lumber. Hold the club against the wood to finish the drill.

WRONG IMPACT

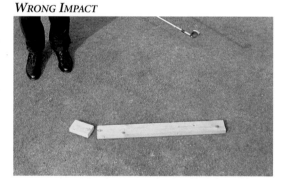

Smooth acceleration was the goal. Instead, too much force from the hands caused a "train wreck."

BREAKING OUT
WORK LIST FOR SUCCESS

1. The lowest point of the swing arc is the target front side of the ball.

2. Except when playing driver or putter, the ball should always be positioned a ball length back from the left armpit.

3. The ball is struck first, but the club must continue down to the lowest point.

4. The hands must lead the clubhead, which tilts the shaft forward, de-lofting the club at impact.

5. Acceleration should always be smooth or you have a train wreck on your hands.

Positive
Practice:
The Pros'
Dynamic
Position
Drills

35

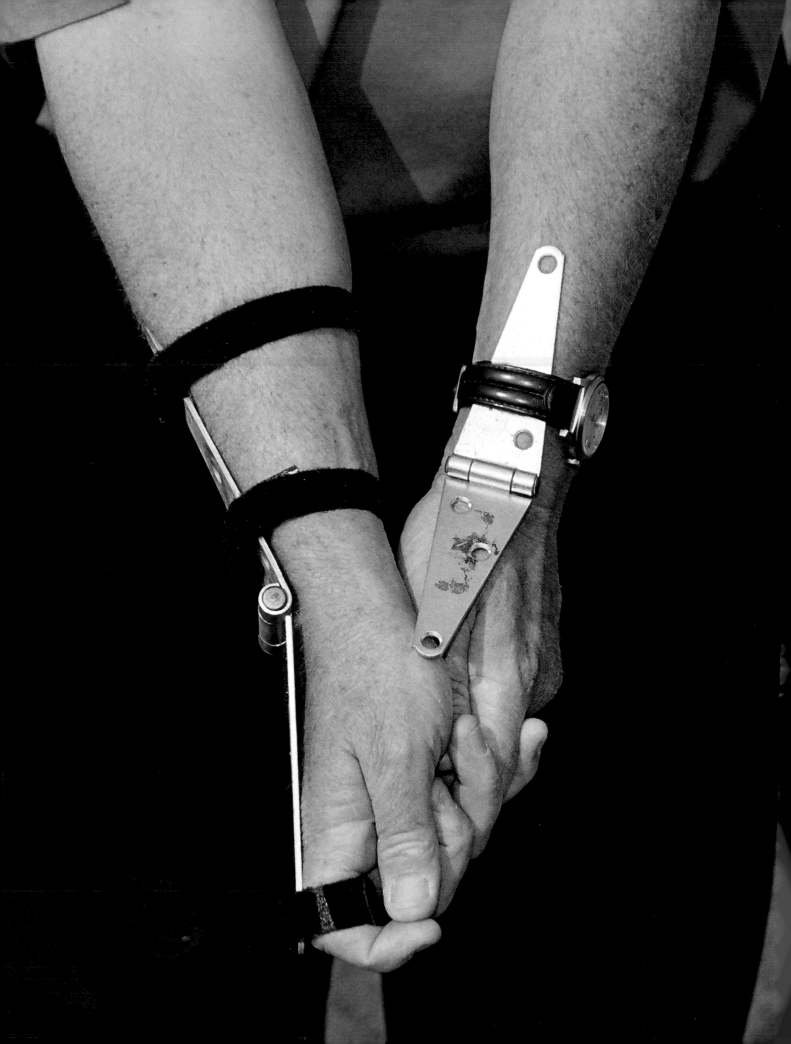

HINGE YOUR WRISTS CORRECTLY

It is no wonder that so many golfers don't understand what their wrists should do during the golf swing. So much has been written about wrists, and in so many different terms, that it is confusing. Confusion leads to misconceptions, which lead to practicing the wrong wrist action. All this conspires to keep you from making the improvement you so desperately want.

From this point on, I suggest you sweep away the cobwebs of wrist action ideas from your brain and focus on the photo at left. Only think of your wrists hinging. To illustrate how each wrist hinges, I will demonstrate with hinges purchased at my local home improvement store.

We will spend a considerable amount of time on correct wrist motion. Though it is quite simple, wrist motion is misunderstood. And until wrist motion is corrected, no improvement in your game is possible.

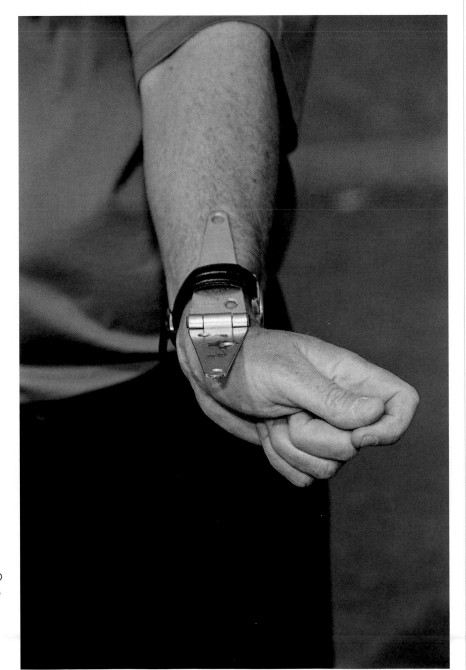

WRIST HINGING

Each wrist hinges in a certain direction. Martin suggests purchasing some inexpensive hinges, like these, along with Velcro straps at your local home improvement store. Practice at home with the hinges mounted on your wrists and train to hinge each wrist in a certain direction.

LEFT WRIST HINGE

If I brought you to the hospital for titanium left wrist hinge implant, it would be placed on the top of your left wrist. This would allow the left wrist to hinge in an up-and-down motion only, and would never allow your left wrist to move back and forth. Back-and-forth motion would be eliminated, which is exactly what you have to eliminate from your golf swing.

UP AND DOWN ONLY

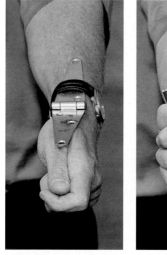
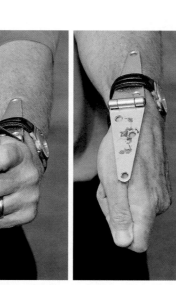
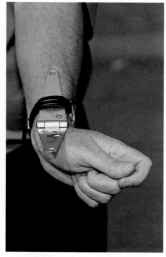

NEVER BACK AND FORTH

If we screwed the left wrist hinge firmly in place, it would not allow the left wrist to move back and forth. The correct

The hinge is on top. The left wrist hinge motion is up and down. If you purchased the hinges and strapped the left one on the top of your wrist, you would find your left wrist would only be able to move up and down.

hinging action must only be up and down. Strapping a hinge on your left wrist will program your swing for the correct way to hinge the wrist.

ANOTHER VIEW

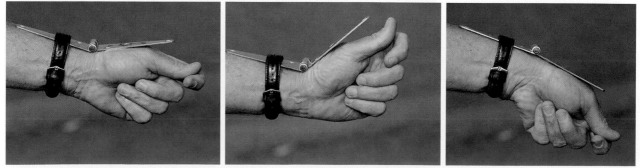

Being able to hinge only your left wrist up and down is so important; let's take a look at it again from a side view to make sure the motion is easy to understand. The hinge is fastened on top of the left wrist. The left wrist can hinge up. The left wrist can hinge down.

Right Wrist Hinge

Both wrists do not hinge alike. Each must hinge in a specific direction, and that becomes very simple to understand and master once you clearly see and feel the correct motion.

While the left wrist has the hinge fastened on top to enable an up-and-down motion, the right wrist needs its hinge on the back of the right wrist. This enables the right wrist only to bend.

Right Wrist Hinging

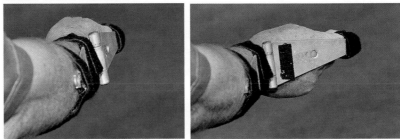

The hinge is on the back. Your right wrist can only hinge by bending.

A hinge placed on the back of the right wrist allows it to only bend, but not cock.

Wrists Working Together

Teamwork

Keeping the hinges attached emphasizes that the wrists are like the members of a great team. Each has its own responsibility in producing a winning effort.

As the photos show, the wrist hinges are in different places on each wrist. For the left wrist, the hinge is on top so the wrist can move up and down. On the right wrist, the hinge is on the back of the wrist so it can bend back and forth.

Right Wrist Bend

As I grip the club, it is already possible to see a slight bend in the back of the right wrist. This bend is very important, and is the subject of some upcoming drills.

Left Wrist Cock

As seen together, the left wrist hinge can be only up and down. As we progress, you will see why that is so important to our goal of attaining a straight line with the left arm and shaft just after impact. If the wrists flipped and bent a straight line would never be possible. This is a prime reason so many golfers simply can't improve. The steel rod connection is the subject in the next drill.

Chalk Talk

"Cock the Wrists" is Wrong:

People who say "you must cock and uncock your wrists," are completely wrong. Only the left wrist should cock up and down. The right wrist shouldn't cock; it should only bend.

Shepherd's Crook Drill

Now you understand the left wrist should only move up and down during the swing. This drill provides a check to make sure the wrist does not incorrectly bend instead. Goal: Training the left wrist not to bend through and past the impact zone.

To illustrate how the right wrist stays bent as the clubhead returns to the ball, try this easy drill.

THE HOOK

I've attached a hook that fits into the top of the grip.

SETUP

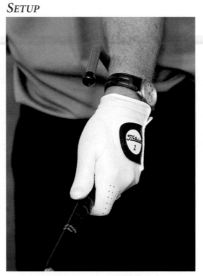

The hook does not touch but is very close to the inside of the left forearm.

GOOD

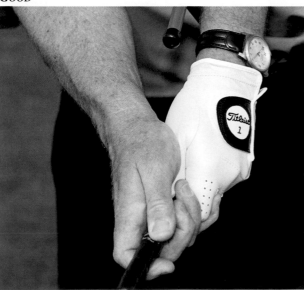

Through impact, the hook now touches the left forearm.

BAD

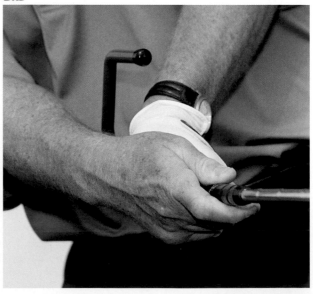

Through impact, the left wrist has incorrectly bent, causing the bar to stay far off the left forearm.

RIGHT WEDGE DRILL

For this drill, the right forearm stays on the wedge at address. As the right wrist bends back on the downswing and as the club approaches the impact area, the wedge and right forearm separate slightly.

THE WEDGE

By inserting a wedge between the shaft and the right wrist, the correct wrist bend: you can easily establish.

GRIP

While still holding the wedge in place, grip the club with your right hand so it extends up the inside of your left forearm.

SET THE WEDGE

With your left hand, position the wedge against the top of the grip.

ADDRESS

When you address the ball, the wedge and the forearm must be touching.

APPROACHING IMPACT

The wedge and right forearm have separated. Notice the slight right wrist bend as the hands are ahead of the clubface. The shaft is tilted foreword and the club is de-lofted. We have achieved our goal.

BREAKING OUT
WORK LIST FOR SUCCESS

1. You will improve by practicing the correct wrist hinges for each wrist.

2. Purchasing inexpensive hinges and Velcro straps will lead to lower scores, if you practice with hinges at home.

3. Only the left wrist cocks up and uncocks down.

4. Only the right wrist bends.

5. The goal is to create and maintain a straight line formed by the left arm and shaft just past impact and continuing to the Check-point Charley position in the follow-through.

6 POSITIVE PRACTICE

Wouldn't it be nice if you could read about changes that need to be made and just like that they became part of your game? Fortunately, you do have the ability to improve, and you will improve. But you have to work at it. The best way to start is with the drills in this chapter.

When you watch the PGA TOUR on television, the players make it all seem so simple with their fluid swings. But every TOUR player has tendencies that can get him into trouble unless he constantly practices to reinforce good positions in his swing. In a TOUR player's case, the practice sessions are defensive. For most middle- and -higher-handicap golfers who are serious about improving, practice sessions should be geared more toward ingraining new habits, new feelings and correct techniques into their games. Practice should be fun, but the key is to practice what helps you.

If you are like most players who want to improve, chances are that improper wrist motion is holding you back. Just reading about how each wrist hinges is interesting, but it won't do you much good unless you practice to make correct hinging part of your game.

The best news is that once you make this a natural part of your game, you will see improvement. You will be striking the ball in the pro style, with more consistency, instead of like a player without a clue who occasionally hits good shots. Practice is worth the effort. But you should only practice with drills that provide positive feedback.

SHAFT CONTACT DRILL

This drill is similar to one we did in an earlier chapter, but as you will see, it is more dynamic. You will find it is fun, simple to do and you can hit a ball.

Start with the shaft against your left side. It should not touch your side again once the swing begins. This drill helps develop a pro's flat left wrist from impact to partial follow-through.

THE GRIP TEE

Use the same grip tee as earlier, with an old grip slipped part of the way up the cut-off butt of the shaft. Insert a tee in the end of the grip and tee up a ball.

GRIP THE SHAFT

Grip the club lower down on the shaft.

SHAFT AGAINST SIDE

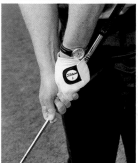

As you set up, the grip should be resting against your left side.

ADDRESS

The ball should be slightly back in your stance so that it is just back of your left armpit. Your grip should be normal but down on the shaft. The club grip should be in contact with your left side.

TAKEAWAY

Only take the club away to a hip-high position on the backswing. Notice the grip has moved away from your left side.

FLAT WRIST AT IMPACT

As the club approaches impact and then through it, my left wrist has not bent. It is flat because, as you learned earlier, it can only move by hinging up and down. Positive feedback that you did this correctly is that the grip of the club must not contact your side. Negative feedback occurs if the grip does slap your side, indicating you bent your left wrist.

SECONDARY SHAFT DRILL

This aid will help you grip the club normally. Use it to hit some short shots. The second shaft provides the feedback. Correct wrist hinging keeps the shaft away from my body through impact and beyond. A caution: You would not want to take a full swing with it.

This drill continues the re-education of the proper wrist hinging action in the golf swing. All of these drills are designed to create the pro's position when it counts the most: through the hitting zone.

ADDRESS

I grip the club normally on the regular grip. The second shaft just touches my body at address because the shaft is more vertical. It must be tilted forward when I swing back, which prevents the second shaft from touching my side.

BACKSWING AND DOWNSWING

A half-swing is all you need. Notice the shaft is extended away from my body. The right wrist bends and the left wrist cocks slightly upward. On the downswing, the weight transfers forward. The left wrist has not bent. The right wrist stays bent. The hands are ahead of the clubhead at impact. The shaft is tilted forward, as it should be.

PAST IMPACT

The flat left wrist keeps the second shaft away from my body.

CHECKPOINT CHARLEY

I have a special name for this position because it is a very important checkpoint in the swing. The secondary shaft is still not touching my body, and that is proof my left wrist stayed flat even to this very important position.

LIE-OF-THE-CLUB DRILL

Another good drill to practice is this one where the lie of the club comes into play. You can program the right feeling when your wrists are in their correct positions at impact.

Purpose: With a target line to interact with on the ground, you will feel what the correct wrist positions are at impact, knowing the sweet spot of the club is directly on the target line.

CLUBFACE SETUP

Attach a magnetic lie angle (available in golf specialty stores) onto the sweet spot of this hybrid iron. The loft is about that of a 2-iron.

ADDRESS

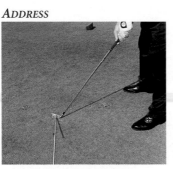

Set up in a normal address position. Align the lie angle, attached to the sweet spot, over a target line placed on the ground.

IMPACT

Change your position to simulate impact while keeping the lie angle still overlapping the target line. Your hands should be forward of the clubhead. Your left wrist should be flat.

SMACK-THE-HAND DRILL

Phil Ritson is a well-respected teaching professional in Orlando, Florida. Phil believes all the best players hit the ball with the heel of the right hand. I agree with this. Phil gave me this drill.

STARTING POSITION

Begin with your palms together held out in front of you.

BACKSWING

Take your right arm back as you bend your right wrist. Remember that the right wrist hinges to the bent position.

SMACK THE PALM

Smack the heel of the right hand into the palm of the left hand while maintaining the bend in the right wrist. Did you notice how your upper body wanted to move through the shot? That is exactly what you want to feel.

CHALK TALK	**HOW A RIGHT WRIST BEND HELPS:**	If you keep your right wrist slightly bent through the hitting area, your body will keep turning. I have found that to be true!

RIGHT WRIST BEND

RIGHT WRIST POWER CLICK DRILL

The Power Clicker offers a telltale signal if you bend your right wrist correctly. It is available online or through golf specialty stores. Here's how the tool works. The right wrist must bend back on the backswing, and that bend must be maintained to some extent through the hitting area. This training aid should click only once.

The positive feedback would be to not hear another click again past impact. The reason: You want to maintain the wrist bend instead of flipping your wrists through the ball.

Here is a pro secret that most amateurs may not be aware of. It deals with the bend that is maintained in the right wrist during the swing. Keep this mental image in mind as you do the next few drills.

ADDRESS **THE ONLY CLICK** **NO CLICK**

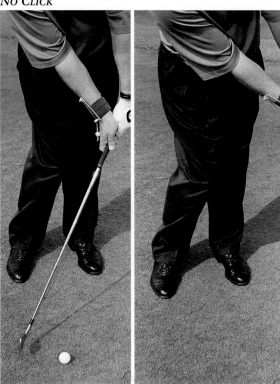

As you address the ball, the Power Clicker should not have clicked.

As the right wrist bends you should hear one click, indicating your wrist has hinged back correctly.

You do not want to hear a second click, which would indicate the right wrist bend has disappeared through the hitting area. Silence is golden.

LEFT WRIST POWER CLICK DRILL

This is a case where the "best news is no news," or rather, the "best news is no sound." The Power Clicker only makes a click when the wrists bend, and, as you have been learning, the left wrist should not bend at all. The left wrist moves up and down but should never move back and forth.

The power clicker detects any bending of the left wrist through the impact zone. This would be negative feedback, and you will instantly know you made a mistake: You will hear a click.

Make a swing. No click should be heard through this entire sequence, starting at address.

Note that the left wrist hinges up but does not break.

At impact the wrist is flat.

Looking at Checkpoint Charlie we see that the wrist is still flat.

CHALK TALK

QUICK REVIEW:

The reason the Power Clicker does not click when it is on the left wrist is that the hinge would be on top. The left wrist should only hinge up and down.

STRAIGHT LEFT ARM SELF-TEST

Try this self-test to verify that your left arm remains straight in line with the shaft through the hitting area of your swing. This is the pro position, and if your wrist hinges are correct, you will immediately see positive results at the checkpoint. If the arms are not in a straight line that means you need to work on improvement.

This drill verifies your progress toward breaking out of whatever has been holding you back. In this case, you're encouraging the straight line formed by the left arm and shaft.

SET UP THE DRILL

Stick a dowel in an old shaft (you can use a long, solid pole). Place a club down by your heel and extend it out. Insert the pole at an angle, as illustrated here.

BACKSWING

A half-backswing is all you need.

DOWNSWING

Just bring the club back nice and easy.

PRE-IMPACT

The left wrist should be flattening now. The right wrist bend should be maintained.

THE SELF-TEST POSITION

The pole serves as a stopping checkpoint area for an abbreviated follow-through. Stop before you reach the pole. If your left arm and shaft form a straight line, you are making great progress. This straight-line relationship should begin right after impact and continue to this point. If the left arm and shaft are not in a straight line, it has to do with what your wrists are doing. A suggestion would be to attach the hinges to your wrists, as we did earlier, and practice slowly with this drill to program the correct feeling of hinging each wrist correctly.

TAKE-UP-THE-SLACK DRILL

Another way to work on the straight left arm and shaft past impact is with this drill. You will need a piece of webbing that is adjustable at the arm; attach the other end to a clamp that fits on the club.

This drill takes up the slack in the attached strap, indicating that the left arm and shaft are in a straight line through the hitting area.

ADDRESS POSITION

With the strap attached to the shaft and the elbow, it should be taut at address. The next time the strap will appear this way is just past impact.

BACKSWING & DOWNSWING: STRAP IS SLACK

The strap should be slack on the backswing, downswing and just before impact. Notice the left wrist position in the sequence. The left wrist hinges upward. Also note the bend in the right wrist as the club enters the hitting area.

IMPACT & FOLLOW-THROUGH: STRAP IS TIGHT

The strap's slack is taken up just past impact when the left arm and shaft form a straight line. This is a pro's power position. Notice the flat left wrist.

GOOD

At follow-through, the shaft and left arm still correctly form a straight line. This is your goal: the ideal pro position!

BAD

This is what most poor players do at Checkpoint Charley: They cross the strap over the shaft by poor wrist positions. With your now—educated vision, you can see how wrong this is.

QUICK REVIEW DRILLS

Many of these drills are similar, and that is a good thing because each adaptation builds on what you are already starting to understand and feel. These drills use the Power Clicker, but you will swing with only one hand on the club.

RIGHT HAND ONE-CLICK DRILL

With the Power Clicker attached to your right wrist, swing back and hear just one click. Then swing down and through. No more clicks should be heard. The reason: The right wrist keeps the bend through the hitting area.

LEFT HAND NO-CLICK DRILL

With the Power Clicker attached to your left wrist, swing back and forth without hearing a click. The wrist does not bend back and forth, which would cause the Power Clicker to tattle on you. Silence indicates the left wrist remianed flat through the hitting area.

BREAKING OUT
WORK LIST FOR SUCCESS

1. Read the chapter on wrist hinging.

2. Hinging your wrists correctly will make all the difference to your game improvement process.

3. Practice the correct wrist hinge positions in a mirror at home. Is your left wrist flat past impact in the mirror?

4. Have you maintained the bend in the right wrist past impact in the mirror?

5. Still using the mirror, simulate the self-test positions shown within the drills.

6. Take your practice to the range but always check and re-check your wrist hinge positions at this stage of the re-learning process.

7. Only practice with drills that provide feedback. You're working too hard on your game to practice the wrong technique.

8. As you progress to the next chapters that deal with other phases of the game, never forget these wrist hinge positions.

9. Out on the course, while you're waiting to tee off or for another shot, refresh your mind about these correct positions.

THE PROS' APPROACH

PGA TOUR players sometimes can't tell you exactly what they do in their swings because they don't "think about it." They are trained to just "do." Like all good players, their just past impact position looks very similar. Just as Martin demonstrates on the swing board (photo left), the left arm and shaft are in a straight line. This position has real value in producing high quality, consistent golf shots for all your clubs. To get to this position, however, you need to begin working on your approach to the ball. You have already learned that the lowest point in the swing is the target side of the ball, a major change in thinking for most players. So, with the exception of driving and putting, the club needs to be on a descending path when it contacts the back of the ball.

Combined with your new pro-style wrist hinges, the approach explained here will have you hitting quality golf shots. The drills in this chapter will help you develop a sense of just how to change your approach to the ball.

TOWEL TRAP DRILL

I like this drill because it focuses your eyes and brain on the ball by limiting the target area. It also provides a narrow piece of turf to swing down toward, helping you trap the ball perfectly. This drill provides immediate feedback. If your swing is descending, you hit the ball; if not, you trap the towel instead.

WHAT YOU NEED

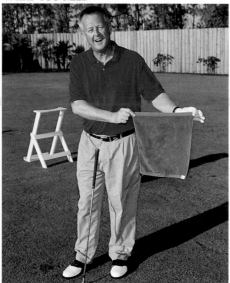

A towel is the perfect size for this drill.

TOWEL POSITION

Smooth out the towel and place it about three inches behind the ball.

ADDRESS

I suggest doing this drill with a 6-iron or 7-iron. Notice how the towel has focused in and limited the hitting area.

TOP OF THE BACKSWING

A three-quarter backswing is what you will need for this shot. Look at how my left wrist has correctly hinged upward. This is called left wrist cock. You can see the bend in my right wrist as it outlines my head in this view.

DOWNSWING A

The key to both of these positions is what my wrists are doing. The left wrist is hinged upward. The right wrist maintains the bend created on the takeaway.

DOWNSWING B

The hands are correctly ahead of the clubhead. The shaft is tilted forward as the club is about to swing over the towel.

The clubhead cleared the towel and is about to impact the ball while still descending. Here is why. The left wrist is flat. The right wrist retains its bend. As a result the hands are ahead of the clubhead. The shaft is tilted forward. And the face has been correctly de-lofted.

The clubhead descended over the towel and is about to impact the ball.

Fans who hang out around the practice range at PGA TOUR events often remark how different the ball sounds when the pros hit it. It sounds crisper because they are trapping the ball and compressing it. Fans also see the range torn up with divots, and you have learned that, to a pro, the club does not stop going down when it impacts the ball. They hit the small golf ball before the big ball—Earth.

Professional golfers and better players make the swing look simple and efficient. Their power is not created by flailing their arms around. It is really created by doing a number of easily learned techniques based on their understanding of what certain swing elements must accomplish.

I just demonstrated what a good descending swing looks like. What happens using the same drill if the wrist angles are not maintained? The results are easily predictable.

STRAIGHT LINE PAST IMPACT

POOR PLAYER POSITION

This example illustrates that a flat left wrist has not been maintained at impact. Notice the bent left wrist. An attached hinge on top of the wrist would never allow that position. The bent wrist

When you hear people talk about wrist release at impact, throw their thoughts out with the rubbish. Here, my wrists have retained their positions; as a result, the straight line of my left arm and shaft exist past impact.

results in the shaft being vertical instead of tilted forward before impact. At impact the ball is scooped instead of trapped. The clubhead is actually swinging up, not down. The clubface loft is increased as a result of the bent wrist.

HIT-THE-STRING DRILL

A small piece of string will help you develop a consistent downward stroke. I placed the towel behind the ball with the idea that you swing down over it. But the string will serve a different purpose. This time you want to hit the string after the ball. Done in combination with the towel drill, a pro's approach is definitely in your future.

This drill makes sure both arms are straight after impact and the club is going downward. Positive feedback is that you will hit the ball and the string. Negative feedback is you will just hit the ball.

Place a piece of string about three inches away from the ball, on the target side of the ball, so you can hit the string after impacting the ball.

ANATOMY OF A DESCENDING HIT

This drill photo sequence shows exactly how a descending hit is achieved. Check the wrist hinge positions and their effect on the shaft and clubhead angle. This is a very positive mental image. The best part is you can easily do this drill yourself.

ADDRESS

Notice that at address the shaft is vertical. When people say that both address and impact are the same, you have another bit of scrap to throw out with the rubbish. The shaft will be tilted forward at impact, not vertical as seen here at address.

PARTIAL BACKSWING

My left wrist hinge is up (cocked), while the shaft is in a parallel to the ground position. My right wrist hinge is in the bent-back position.

DOWNSWING

Both angles are retained. Poor players would have an almost vertical shaft at this point of the swing because of poor hinge positions. My wrist positions are keeping my hands in front of the clubhead. The shaft is tilted forward.

PRE-IMPACT

In this posed pre-impact photo, look at how all angles are the same. My hands are leading the way. The shaft is tilted forward. The clubface is de-lofted. The clubhead is on a downward trajectory.

MISSION ACCOMPLISHED

The ball was hit and the club now hits the string that was resting on the ground. Positive results!

POSITIVE OUTCOME

As a result of good wrist hinge positions, I'm able to achieve the goal: straight arms after impact.

STRAIGHT ARMS AFTER IMPACT POSITION

Other than at address, you can't simply put yourself into correct positions at specific points in your swing. You have to swing into those positions. If they are correct, it is due to your understanding and practice to achieve various elements that led up to these good positions.

The position of straight arms after impact is a result of good wrist hinge practices. If the positions are incorrect there is no conceivable way the club will hit the ball, go into the ground and allow your arms to be straight past impact.

GOOD

With all clubs, straight arms after impact is the goal. All good players can be seen in this position. Poor players are never in this position. (A putter would be the exception to this rule.)

POOR

You have heard of a reverse pivot? This is reverse wrist positions. The arms are not straight because: the left wrist is bent back and is not straight, and the right wrist is straight but is not bent back. As a result, the club does not swing down and through the ball. Rather, the club is swung up through the ball, and distance and accuracy suffers.

CHALK TALK

RELAX, HAVE FUN:

Relax when you do these drills. It's very easy to feel tension when you're trying to succeed, but tension is the golf swing's worst enemy. These drills require good wrist positions to achieve the desired results. Trust these drills because these easily learned wrist positions will turn your game around in a positive direction. So relax and let them work for you.

TOM LEHMAN'S STRAIGHT ARMS

PGA TOUR Partners Club President and 2006 Ryder Cup captain Tom Lehman plays TaylorMade clubs and regularly goes through TaylorMade's MATT system. In this stop-action, computerized, top-down photo of his swing, notice how both arms are straight after impact and his left wrist is flat.

CONSISTENT SHOT PATTERNS

Consistency is important in golf. When you evaluated your game earlier, you didn't evaluate it on just one result. You looked at the results of several shots to see the overall pattern.

The same is true as we work together improving your game. The next drill is one that requires hitting five balls; based on the divots you will see a pattern of where you are at the moment. This is a very good drill to repeat as you progress.

DIVOT POSITION DRILL

In this drill five balls will be lined up in a straight line. You will hit each ball. If the bottom of the swing arc is where it should be, all the divots will be on the target side of the ball line. This drill evaluates your current progress. Positive feedback will be a consistent divot pattern on the target side of the line. Negative feedback comes when there are no divots, or when most of them are behind the ball.

BALL SET-UP A

Place a club on the ground. Place five balls on the target side of the shaft. Tip: Place a tee at each end of the club to mark a reference point of the line.

BALL SET-UP B

Remove the club, leaving the balls in a straight line.

ADDRESS

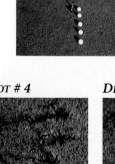

Set up in a good address position with either a 6-iron or 7-iron. The balls should be slightly back of the lowest point of the swing, which is your left armpit. The shaft should be close to vertical at address.

DIVOT # 1

Notice the divot occurred past the ball position.

DIVOT # 2

That's two in a row. Same divot position.

DIVOT # 3

Consistentcy results in lower scores.

DIVOT # 4

Four in a row. The ground is struck after the ball.

DIVOT # 5

You will soon be able to develop the same pattern.

EVALUATING SHOT PATTERNS

Now that the five balls have been hit, we can evaluate where we are on the progress side. Ideally all the divots should start at the same position and all should be on the target side of the shaft.

When you do this drill, it is important to relax. Your brain is a marvelous computer, and the knowledge and feelings you have been programming it with are its reference points. Let it do its job, although you might want to incorporate wrist hinge positions into a pre-shot routine.

POSITIVE FEEDBACK

In this case all my divots are on the target side of the shaft that I returned to the ground. This means all the balls were struck on a downward swing. The club continued into the ground at its lowest point, my left armpit. The ball has left before the clubhead hits the ground in a very good swing.

NEGATIVE FEEDBACK

This is the more common scenario. Divots tend to be all over the place. Some divots indicate the wrists were flipping. Some divots indicate a forced hitting down instead of a natural going down trajectory as s result of correct wrist hinge positions.

REVIEW

The divots should start just slightly ahead of the club. After the club impacts the ball, it goes into the ground where the target side of the ball was. There could be a number of other reasons for this, having to do with address, but the primary reason for the negative feedback shot pattern is improper and inconsistent wrist hinge angles.

If you tried the self-test once and this was your result, it could also be from trying too hard. Do it a few more times until you develop some confidence. That will provide the correct assessment of where you are progress-wise at any given point in time.

CHALK TALK

PRO TIPS:

David Toms and Chris DiMarco are two PGA TOUR players who have incorporated a partial backswing to verify position in their pre-shot routines. For now you might want to consider including the wrist hinge angles from the top of the backswing down to the ball in your pre-shot routine to tweak your brain before actually hitting the ball.

IMAGE AND REALITY

The final two drills in this chapter will continue to help you develop the skill of having your hands lead the clubhead as you maintain the correct wrist hinge positions.

Both utilize the "noodle" that is sold for kids in many stores. What you use to mount the noodle doesn't make a difference as long as the mount will keep it at the correct height.

The first is a reality drill that you can hit balls with, and the second is an image drill that once again creates the very positive mental image for what you need to achieve. Both can be done at home or on the practice range.

BUMP-THE-NOODLE DRILL

This reality drill makes it very easy to feel what you are doing as the club comes back down to the ball.

Goal: The hands need to hit the noodle before the clubface hits the ball. This indicates the shaft is tilted forward prior to impact and that your wrist is flat.

SET THE NOODLE AND ADDRESS THE BALL

LEFT HAND HITS NOODLE

Set up the noodle so it is about three inches ahead of the target side of your hands. The correct height will allow the back of your left hand to touch it.

As you swing or practice, the back of your left hand should bump the noodle before the club hits the ball. A pro will hit the noodle with his hands before the club hits the ball. Notice my left wrist is flat pre-impact. If you do this on the range you can take full swings because the noodle is only foam rubber and you won't hurt yourself. Try videotaping your swing to see which you hit first, the noodle or the ball.

RING-THE-DOORBELL DRILL

Image drills reinforce positive thoughts. Ponder a familiar or humorous swing to describe a specific motion. In this case, instead of wrist hinge, think about ringing the doorbell with the butt of the club.

Purpose: To create positive reinforcement of the correct wrist hinge positions the club reaches at the parallel-to-the-ground position on the downswing.

SET UP THE NOODLE

TOP OF BACKSWING

RING THE DOORBELL

For this drill, set the noodle so that it points back from the target line between your knee and hip. My hand points to where the pointing edge of the noodle needs to be.

You will not be hitting a ball. This drill only works on the correct wrist positions on the way down.

Maintaining correct wrist positions—and not releasing them—will allow you to swing the butt of the club to a point where it touches the edge of the noodle. You just rang the bell for success.

BREAKING OUT
WORK LIST FOR SUCCESS

1. Relax before doing these drills.

2. Allow your brain to do the programming work, but give it prompts.

3. Practice positions at home so they are natural on the course.

4. Incorporate some wrist position features into your pre-shot routine.

5. Take the self-tests frequently to stay sharp and check (or "mark") progress.

8

PROS' GRIP SECRETS

Every pro practices the basics of the game. All good golfers adjust their ball flight to produce quality shots. Even for the world's best, it doesn't take much for their games to get a little off due to compensations they make somewhere in their swing.

The most interesting and informative time to go to a golf tournament is early in the week. Monday especially, when players work hard on various parts of their games. Sometimes it is to correct a swing fault that may have crept in or just to stay sharp, fine-tuning swings that have amateurs salivating with envy.

Pros take drills and training aids very seriously. Even while warming up, they usually practice with a club on the ground for alignment or mirrors to verify certain positions. Their biggest fear is to practice something that is wrong and have that wrong element ingrained in their game.

The photo on the opposite page shows a square clubhead at impact. The clubs on the ground are a simple target alignment aid. Add in a professional grip and you too can send the ball straight to the target. I have a few tips that will eliminate any mistakes that might have crept into your game. I want you to be the best you can be.

CONVENTIONAL GRIP

Most golfers have what we call a conventional grip, which is primarily what we will be working with here. That gives you the best chance of swinging without any unnecessary compensations. True to their unique nature, some TOUR players have made adaptations to this grip to suit their preferences.

Paul Azinger prefers to play with a strong grip while Johnny Miller and Cory Pavin won U.S. Opens with weak grips. Strong or weak are not terms that deal with how hard the club is gripped. They refer to hand positions.

THE HANDS' ROLE IN THE SWING

Most golfers should be neutral-grip players. To have any sort of unusual grip, you have to be very talented to make it work.

The right hand has a lot to do with hitting the ball first and the ground second. The left hand has a lot to do with how accurate your shots are. For example, we spent considerable time dealing with wrist hinge positions. Do you recall that the left wrist must be flat through the hitting zone? That dealt with accuracy to go along with power.

CHALK TALK

HAND:	ROLE:	PRODUCES:
Left	Controls the clubface	Accuracy
Right	Controls the clubhead	Power

LEFT HAND

As we start working on the grip let's start with accuracy first. That means we begin with the left hand.

LEFT HAND GRIP

When you grip the club with your left hand you want to grip it primarily with fingers. The club should go from just under the first knuckle of your left hand to just under the heel pad. I like to call the heel pad the sixth finger.

I know we have four fingers and a thumb, but for simplicity let's say we have five fingers and the heel pad, which makes six fingers. Make sure the sixth finger (the heel pad) is touching the club. That is the way Annika Sorenstam thinks.

LEFT THUMB FIRST

The left thumb should be on the side of the club. You want to give the club a good thumbprint.

UNDERSIDE VIEW

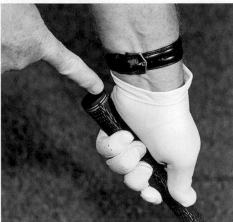

The thumb is on the side. The club is held in the fingers. The heel pad—the sixth finger—is on top.

GRIPPING THE CLUB

There are two good ways to take the left-handed grip. Both work fine, but you should choose one to start building a consistent way to do things.

FIRST

The club   is on the outside of your left foot. Now take your grip with your left arm hanging to your side.

SECOND

Hold the club in your right hand with the shaft vertical. Place the left hand on the club.

ZERO THUMB GAP

There should be no gap whatsoever between the thumb of the left hand and first finger of the left hand. Here is a good way to practice that.

USE A COIN

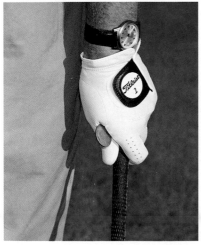

Insert a coin between the thumb and first finger and hold it in place. In this case, I'm holding the coin in my left-hand grip, but neither grip has a gap between the thumb and first finger.

MISTAKES TO AVOID

Here are the two most common errors of a left-hand grip. They are like computer viruses and must be avoided at all costs or they will spread their contamination into all phases of your game. That is not an overstatement; a golf synonym for contamination could be compensation.

GRANDDADDY OF MISTAKES

The deadly palm grip. The grip is incorrectly held in the palm of the hand like a baseball bat.

WIDE-SET THUMB

This also occurs in poor golfers. The thumb decides to go off on its own. Bribe it with that coin to train it to behave and stay close to the index finger.

MY GLOVE TRAINING AID

You know that grungy old glove you have in your bag? It's well past being an effective contributor to your game, so take out a sharpie and turn your glove into a teaching aid.

I've drawn some lines, circles and spots to demonstrate exactly where you want your left hand to go when it grips the club.

FINGER GRIP

Lay the club along the fingers, starting under the first knuckle of the left index finger.

UNDER THE HEEL PAD

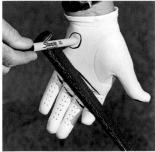

This circle represents the sixth finger. The club should be laid along the fingers under this heel pad position.

ZIP IT UP

Keep the thumb and index finger close together by zipping up the gap. I have drawn zipper teeth on the glove for the mental image. The big thumbprint reminds you that the thumb must make quite a print on the side of the club.

RIGHT HAND GRIP

Now it is time to switch hands and turn our attention to the right hand. The right hand holds the swing's power because it controls the clubhead. The left hand is for accuracy; the right hand is for power.

THE 'V' POINTS HERE

Point the 'V' formed by the thumb and index finger to just between your chin and your right shoulder.

Before you grip the club with your right hand, there are a few things to consider. You can also make use of the mental images to help you grip it consistently every time.

FINGERS

Just as you do with the left hand, you want the right hand to grip the club in the fingers, not in the palm. The two fingers and thumb, seen in this photo, are the big three for the right hand grip.

NEVER IN THE PALM

Avoid this problem. You are playing golf, not tossing a shot put. Never hold the club in the palm of your right hand.

ADD THE RIGHT

Once you followed the keys to gripping the club correctly with the left hand, it is time for the right. I firmly believe you need to develop a firm way of doing things in setting up to hit the ball to produce quality shots consistently.

Nothing happens until you swing, so you have ample time to set up properly. Having a repeatable way to grip the club is a huge asset. Your hands are your body's only direct link to the club, and so much can go wrong if you don't grip correctly.

STEP #1

After gripping the club correctly with your left hand, extend the club out horizontally about waist high.

STEP # 2

Place the middle of your right-hand fingers underneath the club.

STEP # 3

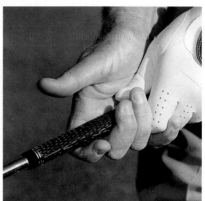

Close the lifeline of your right hand over your left thumb.

ZIP THE GAP

Just as you did with the left hand, you want to zip up the 'V' of the right hand so it is not apart.

The 'V 'of the right hand should also be pointing somewhere between the chin and right shoulder. Both hands' Vs' should be parallel and pointing between the chin and the right shoulder.

GAP CHECK

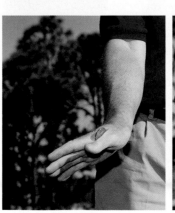

Once again, a gap should not exist between the V of either hand. Your hands need to be zipped up. Use the coin to make sure. You don't want to ruin your game because you can't hold onto your pocket change.

DAVIS LOVE SR. DRILL

Davis Love III learned the game from one of the best teachers of the day—his late father, Davis Love Sr. He showed young Davis a good way to make sure to place the right hand on the club correctly every time.

Start by addressing the ball with both hands on the club.

Allow the right hand to come off the club.

Bring the right hand back to the club to the point where you feel the palm is on the side.

When you close the grip you should feel: The club is in the fingers. The fingers are underneath the club. The palm is on the side of the club.

CHALK TALK

CHECKPOINT:

The palms of both hands should be parallel.

The back of the left hand should (more or less) be facing down the fairway toward your target.

A Matter of Choice

At this stage, you have some leeway to choose which of three grips works best for you. None of them change what has already been accomplished. It is just a matter of what the right-handed pinky does. The three grips are:

- Overlap Grip

- Interlocking Grip

- Ten-Finger or Baseball Grip

OVERLAP GRIP

The pinky of the right hand sits between the index and middle finger of the left hand. I don't suggest you just lay the finger on top of the finger. I suggest placing it under the left index finger knuckle.

INTERLOCKING GRIP

Who uses this grip? Tiger Woods and Jack Nicklaus to name a few. The grip is the same as the overlap with one exception: Instead of overlapping, the right-hand pinky is inserted between the index and middle finger and interlocks with the index finger. The key to this grip is no gaps between any of the fingers. The only exception is the right index finger, another secret the pros understand.

BAD INTERLOCK

Avoid this mistake. You could call it the inter-anywhere because the fingers are all over the place.

Trigger Finger

If you look closely at a PGA TOUR player's grip, you will see the gap between the index and middle finger of the right hand. Call it the trigger finger if you wish.

This is the only finger that has any space between it and its neighbor. Think about throwing a ball with your right hand and how you would need to separate the index finger to put any power in your throw.

SET THE GAP

In this overlapping grip, see the gap between the index and middle fingers of the right hand.

TRIGGER-FINGER PLACEMENT

When you put the right-hand index finger on the club, don't have it glued next to the middle finger. The separation allows you to put the index finger knuckle behind the club shaft. The knuckle does not go under the shaft; it goes on the back.

CHALK TALK

AIRTIGHT AND NO GAPS:

A positive grip on the club requires that all the fingers, other than the right index finger, be together regardless of the grip you choose. All the grips have one thing in common: the role of the right-hand index finger.

Davis Love Sr. gave me another tip to eliminate air pockets in the grip. He said to imagine covering the handle with glue and then putting your hands on it. That would get rid of all the air pockets. But that is not to say you want tension when you grip. You just want to eliminate the feeling of air pockets.

Pros' Grip Secrets

GRIP PRESSURE POINTS

When we refer to grip pressure it's easy to get confused about what is trying to be explained. There is grip pressure that refers to how hard you grip the club, and for now let's just say to hold the club lightly. But that is not the grip pressure we are working on at the moment.

The grip pressure I'm referring to now involves the three pressure points in the grip. In a really good swing, you would be able to sense these three pressure points as you move into the hitting area. You don't have to think of all three. You could just think of one, but all three are better. In photo form here they are.

PRESSURE POINT

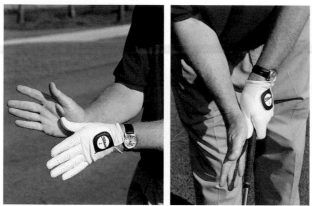

The palm of the right hand and the thumb of the left hand.

PRESSURE POINT

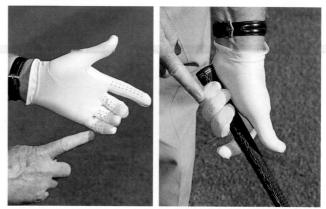

The last three fingers of the left hand and the handle (grip) of the club.

PRESSURE POINT

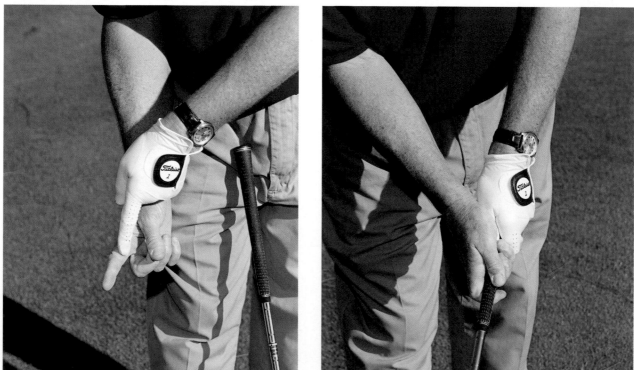

The trigger finger of the right hand against the handle (grip) of the club.

KNOW YOUR 'Vs'

The grip you've been working on (in this chapter) is called a neutral grip. It is neutral because the 'Vs' of both hands are pointing in between the chin and right shoulder. Most golfers are best off playing with this grip.

There are a few variations that some of the best players in the world use, and I'll demonstrate them. However, it takes a lot of talent to master them and accomplish the shots you really want to hit.

OVERLY WEAK GRIP

Johnny Miller and Cory Pavin won U.S. Opens with this grip.

OVERLY STRONG GRIP

Paul Azinger has won a lot of tournaments with this, including the PGA Championship.

While some pros are successful using these variations by choice, many poor players have no clue this is the grip they are using by mistake, not out of design. The neutral grip is your best bet for increased distance and accuracy.

The overly weak grip features the hands overly rotated so that the 'Vs' now point between the chin and left shoulder. This grip requires a lot of hand and wrist action through the hitting area.

If you play this grip you will find it very difficult to draw the ball. On the other hand, you might become a very good iron player and your drives will be fairly straight with some leaking to the right. You will never be a power hitter. You must use your hands to get the club back to square to the target line at impact.

The overly strong grip features the hands rotated to the right so the 'Vs' point past the right shoulder. It requires a definite absence of clubface rotation through the hit. You have to block or hold it off. You will have trouble fading the ball and hitting it high.

BREAKING OUT
WORK LIST FOR SUCCESS

1. Take the time to grip the club correctly every time.

2. Check out the positions in the book in a mirror at home.

3. Hold the club lightly.

4. Hit some practice shots and try to feel the three pressure points.

5. Because this is new, always check to make sure your trigger-finger knuckle is on the back of the club.

9

THE PROS' POSTURE

Tom Lehman has enjoyed a long and successful career highlighted by his 1996 British Open victory at Royal Lytham & St. Annes and his selection as captain of the 2006 U.S. Ryder Cup team. As you look at his posture (left), captured by the sophisticated TaylorMade MATT system, you can easily see what good posture is all about. Tom has set very good angles at address, angles that he can maintain during the swing.

It has been written that a good golf posture is like that of a quarterback taking a snap from center. That is hardly the position you see Tom in at address.

As you look at Tom's posture, the one obvious trait is bending from the hips with only a slight flex in the knees. This is a good athletic position for a golfer! The pros all know this, and at the end of this chapter if poor posture has been holding you back, you will be breaking out of that rut toward improvement.

Posture's Role in the Swing

Posture definitely influences what happens in the swing. The angles you create at address either help to maximize clubhead speed or minimize it. Ideally, you want to be bent forward so the body is about 90 degrees to the angle of the shaft. Things rotate fastest when they go to 90 degrees from their axis.

Bending forward too much causes problems. And not bending forward enough also causes problems. Then there is the sideways bend to the spine. Of course, balance is what we are after. Many golfers think taking a bow will give them the proper bend forward. But the moment you do that you become very much out of balance.

You want to set up like many of the best players. There are some really good players with crappy posture: Colin Montgomerie, Jack Nicklaus, the late Moe Norman and Paul Azinger to name a few. But the odds are in your favor if your posture is good.

Flex comes to mind when posture is discussed. Want a simple rule of thumb for the proper amount of flex in your address position? Your weight-bearing joints should all be in line. This means your knees have been unlocked from a straight position. Too much knee flex and you can come over the top.

SERGIO'S IMPROVED POSTURE

Sergio Garcia has done a lot of work on his swing over the past few years, starting with posture. The TaylorMade MATT system is able to show before and after postures and place them side by side throughout the swing. The new Sergio is silver

- Sergio now stands more upright.
- He has eliminated some knee flex from the past.
- He is more balanced.
- His shoulders are parallel to the target line compared to the slightly opened position he had before.

Imaginary Wall

To get into good posture, develop a mental image of a wall that is about six inches behind your heel line.

You want to stick your butt back to the "wall" line. As your butt touches the imaginary wall, just flex your knees a little, get yourself balanced and then look down at the ball.

Stand up straight with the club held at a slight angle in front of you.

Push your butt back until it touches the imaginary wall, about six inches off your heel line.

Flex your knees slightly while maintaining a balanced feeling. Now place the club on the ground.

KNEE FLEX

How much should you flex your knees? How much is a little? How much is too much? Try this very simple method for determining what works best for you.

IDEAL KNEE FLEX

Hold your club against your chest. Put it in line with your right knee. Flex to a point where the knee just touches the shaft.

CHALK TALK

POSTURE ROUTINE:

A good suggestion is to develop a good posture routine before you hit any shot, even in practice. Once you automatically get yourself into the correct posture, then you can phase it out. To break out of what may be holding you back, you must leave nothing to chance.

DON'T BOW

To break out of the problems that are holding you back, you have to discard old swing thoughts that are totally wrong. Bowing at address is definitely wrong, and here is why.

POOR POSTURE BY BOWING

Standing up straight and just bowing over creates too much top-heavy weight forward, which prevents you from achieving the balance needed to improve.

COURSE BARSTOOL

If you want another mental image, to go along with the imaginary wall, try this one as well. Visualize a barstool, and when you push your butt back, you will be sitting on the stool.

BARSTOOL POSTURE DRILL

Begin by standing upright with a vertical club in front resting on the ground. Push your butt back until it rests on the imaginary barstool. You should feel a little pressure in the front of your thighs.

STABILITY, NOT MOVEMENT

The reason I disagree with the quarterback analogy for posture is that you do not want to be on the balls of your feet. Golf is a stability sport, not a movement sport like tennis or football.

Your arms will whirl from behind your body to out in front of your body on the downswing. I believe the weight should be on the heels. Your arms weigh about 15 pounds each, not including the weight of the club. On the backswing, you are taking a 30-pound weight (your arms), plus whatever the club weighs, behind your body.

This 30-pound-plus weight now has to go rapidly from behind your body to out in front of your body. That will pull you forward. With having the weight on your heels, you have effectively installed a counterbalance.

Balance during the golf swing needs to be geared for stability instead of motion. Golf is not football or basketball.

WIGGLE YOUR TOES

To set up the counterbalance of having the weight on your heels: Start with your weight evenly balanced on your feet. Shift the weight back on your heels. You should be able to wiggle your toes.

FEEL THE BALANCE DRILL

His great sense of humor as a TV analyst makes some people forget that Nick Faldo has won six major championships. A very serious man on the practice tee, Faldo has used drills to keep all facets of his game sharp. When it came to balance, Faldo would practice in his socks so he could feel the correct balance.

At the Masters one year, knowing it was going to continue raining the next day, Faldo took off his socks and stood in the muddy practice range hitting balls to feel what the balance would be to give him the needed stability from a wet surface. Try his drill to feel your balance points.

SHOES OFF DRILL

On occasion, I really feel it is worthwhile to practice without your golf shoes. The full swing requires swinging the weight of your arms along with the club (30-plus pounds) from behind you to the front.

The weight back on your heels provides an anchor, a counterweight to this motion. Golf is a stability game, and maintaining your balance during the swing allows you to reach the hitting area with a pro's approach.

When I have students do this, sometimes they scrunch their toes up and grab the ground like a vulture grabs its prey. That is the wrong feeling. You should be able to wiggle your toes, not grab a piece of meat.

BREAKING OUT
WORK LIST FOR SUCCESS

1. Throw out all past thoughts about posture.

2. Work on a pro's posture.

3. Temporarily develop the pro's posture routine.

4. Practice with a wall at your back.

5. Learn to feel where your weight is during the swing and get it back on your heels.

PROS' SPINE ANGLE AND BALL POSITION

The before and after computer images of Sergio Garcia (left) show different spine tilts as a result of changes he made in his game. Technology has made huge advances, and this TaylorMade MATT program can show players from all views, including this one looking down.

The reason for Sergio's spine tilt change is significant, and how your spine should be positioned like the pros' is the subject of this chapter. Biomechanics has taught us that if your spine is tilted at least five degrees away from the target and not more than 10 degrees, you have a good chance to turn properly and come into the ball at the correct angle and the correct direction.

Our goal is to have you set up with a spine tilt that has the bottom of your spine closer to the target than the top of the spine. This improves your chance of swinging the club back to the ball in a position square to the target line.

The younger Sergio (red) had a reverse spine tilt because, as you can see, the tilt line is farther away from the target at the base. Today's Sergio (silver) may not quite be at the desired five-degree angle, but his position represents vast improvement.

PRO SPINE TILT

Here are both good and bad examples of spine tilt. Observing them from the back view is a good way to learn. As you develop an educated eye as to what to look for, playing with your friends will take on new meaning.

AVOID THE Y TILT

A 5 to 10-degree spine tilt is desirable, but this tilt is in the wrong direction. Instead of the base of the spine being closer to the target than the top, this position reverses the tilt. This tilt has the base of the spine farther from the target line than the top.

FIVE-DEGREE K

This is our goal position. The spine tilt is closer to the target at the base of the spine than it is at the top. The K setup is neutral, which provides the best chance of hitting the ball straight. If the K spine tilt is good, and all biomechanics models agree, then the Y spine tilt is bad. The problems the Y tilt causes are: You slice, you pull or you come over the top.

BALL POSITION

Where the ball is positioned in your stance has a lot to do with the direction it ends up in after you hit it. Ball position is another area we just can't leave to chance. Its location is vital to improvement.

TOM LEHMAN'S BALL POSITION

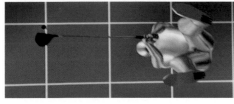

Even on TV you have never seen a view like this. Looking up at Tom Lehman is possible with the TaylorMade MATT system. The computer cameras and sensors Tom wore turned him into a 3D figure, and the view can be rotated 360 degrees. Later in the book you will find how this type of technology can improve your game.

PINPOINTING THE CORRECT POSITION

For right handed-golfers, the common belief is that the ball should be positioned relative to the left foot. Unfortunately, that is not the best way to do it, so toss that old swing thought out in the rubbish along with the others we have discarded to help you improve. It is far more precise to look at ball position relative to your left armpit and left shoulder.

This ties in with the low point of your swing, which we worked on earlier. With a driver you want the ball positioned at the low point of the swing, which is the middle of the left shoulder or the left armpit.

Using three clubs will help you find the exact position for your ball. Whenever you practice, make sure the ball is positioned correctly.

MARTIN'S FOOLPROOF BALL POSITION LOCATOR

Place a club (A) along the ground parallel to the target line. Place another club (B) at a 90-degree angle that you will adjust to the correct ball position. Hold a club (C) from your left armpit.

PERFECT POSITION

The ball is precisely positioned in the lowest part of the swing arc— under my left armpit.

LEFT HEEL FALLACY

In the photos at left, with a normal width stance, the ball might be located near the left heel. But if your stance is wide, the ball position would still be under the left armpit, not by the wider-spaced left foot.

THE PROOF

I'm not advocating your stance should be this wide, but some players, like Allen Doyle and Moe Norman, have been known to extend out this far. As you can see, the ball is still under my left armpit, not my left heel.

Ball Position from Driver to Wedge

The data that deals with today's drivers suggests that manufacturers want the swing to be going up after impact so the ball can launch at a 16-degree angle. You will learn more about that later in this book. But that can be misinterpreted by golfers who don't have a technical expert standing at their side explaining what "swinging up after impact" means.

When you tell golfers to hit up, they assume you mean an action on their part. That results in flipping the wrists trying to help the ball in the air or positioning it farther forward in the stance. Both are poison pills. Want to keep it simple? Do exactly what you have learned here.

- Tee the driver at the lowest point of your swing, opposite your armpit.

- If that is the lowest point, the club has to swing upward automatically after the ball has been hit.

- You will be able to maintain the correct wrist hinge angles.

- You can power through the hitting zone with your arms extended out straight.

- You will be able to have the steel rod straight-line relationship with your left arm and wrist with the shaft.

- Simple is better.

ALL CLUBS BALL POSITION

Left to Right: Wedge, 7-iron, driver. The driver is at the lowest point of the swing. The club will normally start upward after impact. The 7-iron and wedge positions are behind the lowest point in the swing. The clubs will hit the ball before going into the ground.

PROBLEM ALERT:
BALL TEED TOO FAR FORWARD

Should the ball be teed up, as this ball is, ahead of the low point in the swing arc, the swing tendency will be an out-to-in swing unless compensations are made. The ball will start to the left and then pull or slice.

BALL STARTS TO THE LEFT

Notice how the clubface is aimed at the club that was on the ground instead of the target line. This is the position of a ball teed too far forward.

BALL TOO FAR BACK

In this case, the ball is teed too far back in the stance for a driver, behind the lowest point of the swing. The swing will be down. The club will want to swing more inside to outside as compensation from the brain. Pulls and hooks will be the result.

BREAKING OUT
WORK LIST FOR SUCCESS

1. Add the spine tilt to your pre-shot posture routine to program familiarity. It's easy to forget without a routine.

2. Check this position in the mirror at home to burn it into your mind and body.

3. Tee your ball up and take your stance. Do a self-test to check its exact position compared to what you have learned in this chapter.

4. With the ball teed up correctly, slowly make a practice swing, stopping at impact; check your positions, especially your wrists.

5. Do the same with the 7-iron and wedge at their respective correct ball positions.

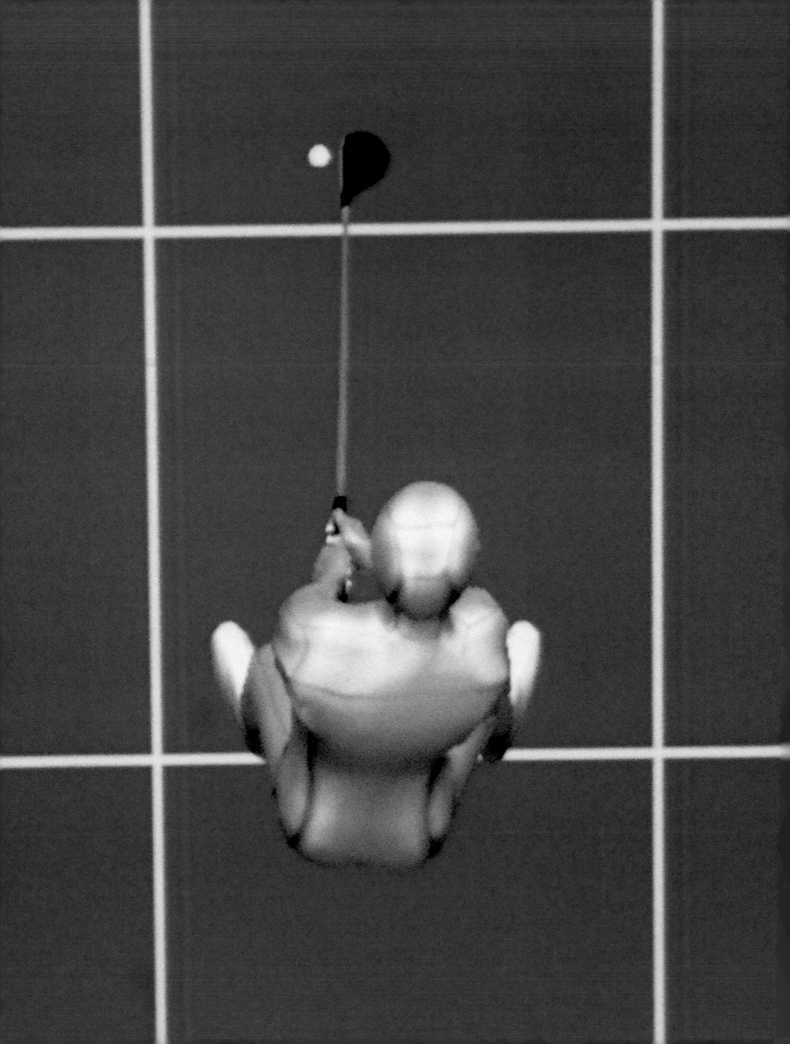

THE PROS' FINER POINTS

PGA TOUR player Fred Funk loves his role as the underdog. In 2005 Funk enjoyed his best season on the PGA TOUR, earning more than $2.8 million, winning THE PLAYERS Championship and running away with The Skins Game.

The computerized view of Fred's address position show some of the fine-tuning, based on some individual needs, that this chapter covers. A blimp's eye view, via the TaylorMade MATT system, allows a unique view of Fred's foot flair, posture bend angle, distance of hands away from the body, head position and tilt.

All these factors present a menu for you to choose from to best suit your individual needs. But remember you can't choose every item on each menu. The explanations and the advantages of each will be demonstrated so you can become an informed selector.

FOOT FLARE

Foot flare has nothing to do with stylish golf shoes. But foot flare is an enormous help when it comes time to turn. The amount of flare means how much the foot is turned out from pointing directly at the target line. You need to know what happens when foot flaring becomes part of your address position.

Most golfers will benefit from having each foot flared out about 10 degrees. But there is a menu of individual preferences for you to select from. The idea is to get the odds for playing consistently good golf in your favor.

You have a menu of possible foot flares to choose from. Be selective. If you slice the ball do not choose from the fixing the hook items in the menu.

So how do you know if you should add some flare to your stance? If your pro tells you that your legs move too much on the backswing, or if your ball flight hooks too much, or if you have seen on video that your hips aren't rotating through the hitting area, you need foot flare. This group of photos pertains to the left foot flaring out from the normal 10 degrees. Each photo will show the adjustment, flare and how it helps.

STANDARD FOOT FLARE

This is the normal, unadjusted position at address. Notice how the toes of each foot point toward the shaft, with an equal flare of about 10 degrees each.

LEFT FOOT FLARED DOES THIS

A flared left foot helps your hips move through the ball. It also helps limit over-rotating of the hips on your backswing. This flair also encourages more coil as you swing back, and encourages more rotation when you swing through the ball. A flared left foot also helps fight a hook.

RIGHT FOOT FLARED DOES THIS

A flared right foot encourages backswing rotation. Senior players can turn back easier when using this foot flare. A flared right foot also helps correct slicing problems.

BALANCE

Think of balance in terms of where the weight is relative to your weight-bearing joints. Balance is a straight line extending from the balls of your feet, your knees and the top of your spine.

LINED-UP BALANCE

When I hold a club from my shoulders, it touches my knees and goes to the balls of my feet.

TOO BENT OVER

Here my trunk is too far forward. The club can't touch my knees and hovers over the grass, not my feet.

TOO FAR BACK

The hanging club proves the balance point is too far back. It is behind my knees instead of touching them.

THE JUMPING BUNNY DRILL

The ability to stay in balance is a common thread running through every skilled golfer's swing. You don't have to be a pro to stay in balance. It's something you can develop and this drill is a good start. An easy to remember reference is to jump into the air like the Easter Bunny.

LOWER YOUR BODY

Starting from a balanced address position, lower your body.

MAINTAIN BALANCE, BEGIN SPRING

Maintain the balance point, spring into the air.

SPRING INTO AIR

Can you spring higher than I can?

LAND IN SAME POSITION

Land in the same position. The landing is important. You should land in the very same place you jumped from. If you are not in balance you won't be able to do it two or three times.

DISTANCE FROM THE BALL

There isn't a golden rule for how far you should stand away from the ball at address. There are golfers, even pros, who stand a long way away and play very well. On the other hand, the legendary Byron Nelson was fond of saying, "You can't stand too close to the ball." As a guideline, and as you work toward consistency, my suggestion is a one-hand span between the top of the grip to your right thigh. The club you use will not make any difference.

ONE-HAND WIDTH

A good guideline for the distance you should stand from the ball is to place the club by the ball with its correct lie angle. Place your hand between the top of the grip and your right thigh (inset). This is the guideline distance regardless of the club being played.

Elbows Down During the Swing

A good mental image is one where your elbows always point down during any phase of the swing. They should never point sideways.

ELBOWS DOWN

I'm holding my arms out for the mental image I want to impress. The elbows should always point down during the swing. They must never point sideways. This item is not a menu choice. Think of it as a mandatory golf-day vitamin.

Chin Position

Time for a quiz. Which of the following pictures is the correct position for the chin as you set up to the ball?

POSITION 1

Is this the correct position? I'm keeping my head down like everyone says.

POSITION 2

Perhaps this is the correct chin position. There is plenty of room here for the shoulders to swing under.

POSITION 3

What do you think of this chin position? The answer to this quiz should be easy.

THE WINNER - #3!

Looking too far down is bad (position 1), and so is having your chin too high (position 2), which is unnatural. Position 3 is a more natural chin position that allows the shoulders to swing under the chin without bumping into it on the backswing.

HEAD TILT

Follow this standard guideline: Keep your head in a position that will keep your eyes parallel to the target line. Some players like Fuzzy Zoeller do change this a bit because of their individual eyesight, but that usually refers only to putting.

PARALLEL TO THE TARGET

Take your address position and hold your club so that it is parallel to your target line. Make sure your shoulders are parallel before continuing

RAISE CLUB TO EYE LEVEL

Raise the club to eye level. It should be held horizontally across both eyes and pointing parallel to the target line.

BACK NOT STRAIGHT

Another golf myth—although this is more of a mini-myth—is that the back should be straight at address. I have even seen a club placed along the backline that goes from the base of the spine and touches the back of the head. That is completely unnatural, so forget it. The head is lower than that club line.

GOOD BACK POSITION

The club goes up the spine but does not touch the back of the head. This position can be maintained during the swing because it's natural.

BAD BACK POSITION

If you were in a full-body cast this might be a natural position, but that would be the only way you would ever be this rigid.

BREAKING OUT LIST
WORK LIST FOR SUCCESS

1. Determine whether foot flare can help your game.

2. Set a club down to verify the degree of flare.

3. Balance is very important in golf. Never take it for granted. Golf is a game of stability, so feel your balance and make sure it's in line.

4. Check your normal chin position in a mirror at home.

5. Work to make all your address positions natural when you're at home so when you go to the practice tee you can work on dynamic golf instead of taking the time working on static positions.

12

PROS' PIVOT DRILLS

One quick glance of the raw power being generated and unleashed in Bubba Watson's swing (at left and below) reveals the real origin of his power: his body rotation. He goes way beyond parallel in the backswing, like John Daly, but those arms and the club are really being powered by the body.

Think of it in terms of a helicopter. The blades, just like the arms in a golf swing, whirl around, but something has to be powering them. The helicopter is powered by an engine and the golf swing is powered by the body pivot. The way you pivot back and forth determines how the power will be built up, stored and then unleashed.

Power has ways of leaking away, so you have to watch very carefully to prevent that from happening. How does power leak away? Sliding instead of pivoting is one problem. To avoid sliding and several other problems, practice the pivot drills in this chapter.

Mirror Drill #1

Some of the best teaching aids you have are right at home. A full-length mirror provides a view of key elements of your golf swing, two of which are the address position and swing motion.

ADDRESS

My range mirror is a little weather beaten by Florida's hurricanes but still provides a very good reflection that you should be looking for in your mirror at home. Put yourself into a good golf athletic position. Cross your hands and place them on the opposite shoulders. Now we will look at some key positions during the swing.

BACKSWING

On the backswing, the left shoulder should appear to be over your right foot.

DAN FORSMAN

The drills in this chapter are designed to produce the hitting zone positions that pros have long understood but most golfers never knew about. Dan Forsman has won five times on the PGA TOUR, and he demonstrates exactly what you need to achieve for improving your game.

Past impact, his left arm has that steel rod relationship with the shaft. His left wrist is flat, and the shaft is tilted toward the target. There are no wasted motions in a pro's swing. Everything pros do is smooth. Working on the body rotation movement drills in this chapter will have you moving down the pro's side of the road toward significant game improvement.

POOR FOLLOW-THROUGH

The mirror revealed a follow-through flaw. The right shoulder should be over the left foot, but as the photo reveals, it is incorrectly in the center of my stance. The mirror allows you to detect problems that creep in unknowingly, which result in compensations you don't realize you are making.

MIRROR DRILL #2

There are several variations of the mirror drill that train and verify the new feeling you're trying to create. This is a good drill to also work on at home if your practice range does not have a mirror.

PUT SHAFT ON NECK

I am using a small section of PVC pipe for illustration purposes, but you can use a golf shaft. First, place the shaft on the back of your neck. Then extend the arms out as you hold it. Bend from the waist after pushing your butt back, and assume a good golf athletic position.

BACKSWING DRILL

Rotate back so that your back points toward the target. Resist the turn with the lower body. Feel the upper body coiling as it rotates. Feel the weight on the right side of the body. Coil to build energy that will be released on the downswing.

FOLLOW-THROUGH DRILL

Initiate the body rotation toward the target with the lower body. Feel the weight transfer from the right side to the left. Your finish position finds your chest facing the target or even left of it.

LOOSEN THE TRUNK

You can't expect to swing freely if your trunk is tight. All golfers, regardless of their skill level, must loosen up before attempting to hit a ball. The key is to loosen up while at the same time instilling a good rotational motion into the warm-up.

SHAFT INSIDE ELBOWS

Pros like to do this drill as a warm-up to loosen up the trunk. Place the shaft on your back but held in place by your elbows. As with the other mirror drills, put yourself in a good golf athletic position.

BACKSWING

You should feel a stretching feeling as you rotate to a position with your back facing the target. Notice my left heel is lifting slightly as the weight transfers over to the right side.

FOLLOW-THROUGH

Rotate back toward the target. Your chest should be pointing at the target. Notice that my right heel is off the ground as the weight has now transferred over to my left side.

PIVOT, DON'T SLIDE

A pro pivots when he swings. Pros don't slide through as higher handicap players do. Pivoting keeps the swing loaded with power so the ball can be walloped through impact. Sliding is an ineffective waste of swing energy. This drill requires a nine-foot piece of rope that is held in the ground by a hook or eye that is pounded in. It needs to be secured because to develop the feel for pivoting you will be pulling on the rope.

SETTING UP

Stand so the hook holding the rope is centered relative to your body. The arms will be out farther than they would normally be.

BACKSWING PIVOT

Pull the right side back. The right shoulder will go back away from the ball.

FOLLOW-THROUGH PIVOT

Pull with the left side. The left shoulder will go back away from the ball. You pivoted instead of sliding. Repeat this drill several times.

LOWER BODY PIVOT DRILL

This drill helps your lower body understand what pivoting should feel like. The key sense to have is that the club, positioned on the back of your thighs, stays level to the ground while you turn.

SHAFT BEHIND THIGHS

Behind your body, place a shaft level across the top of your thighs. Extend your hands slightly outside your bodyline to hold it in place.

ADDRESS

Put yourself into a good golf athletic position. Hold the shaft in place against your thighs. Your feet should be flared just slightly about 10 degrees.

BACKSWING

Pivot back and feel the shaft remaining level. Keep the shaft firmly on the thighs to limit the amount of lower body rotation. In the mirror drill photos, compare this lower body rotation with that of the upper body that rotates to the position where your back faces the target.

FOLLOW-THROUGH

While still keeping the shaft held tightly to the top of the thighs, pivot to a follow-through position. It may not be reality, but it is good to feel that you are keeping the shaft level to the ground as you pivot. Note that your belt buckle, along with your chest, should face the target.

Pros' Pivot Drills

BASKETBALL DRILL

Using a basketball will help instill the feeling of the lower body resisting while the upper body continues turning. This is crucial to producing a swing like the pros. If you have suffered from reverse pivot, where the weight incorrectly goes forward on the backswing and back on the downswing, this is strong medicine that will help correct that problem.

ADDRESS

In all these drills it is important to simulate your address position so you learn to develop a sense of feel for the new and improved swing you are developing. So set up in a good golf athletic position. Hold the basketball between your knees. Place your arms across your chest with your elbows down.

BACKSWING

Turn back while keeping the basketball firmly between your knees. Your shoulders should be rotated back so that your elbows are now over an imaginary table.

WALL DRILLS

Just like the mirror, rope, pivot and basketball drills, you can do this series of drills at home in your spare time. The time spent working on your swing at home will pay huge dividends when you take your game to the range or golf course. If you are like most golfers, your actual time to practice is limited, so working at home is a big improvement booster.

WALL DRILL #1

This drill starts with your back to the wall. The idea is rotating back and through, then touching the wall with the hand on the opposite side of the body.

BACKSWING

FOLLOW-THROUGH

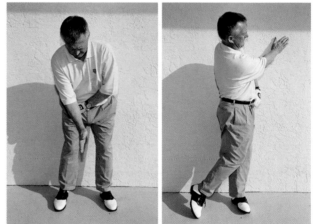

Begin by standing with your back six inches from the wall. Get into a good golf athletic posture. Place your right arm on your waist, and extend your left hand down in front of your left hip. Pivot so that you touch the wall with your left hand.

At the address position, place your right arm across your waist, and extend your left arm down in front of your right hip. Pivot and touch the wall with the palm of your right hand.

FORWARD-BEND WALL DRILL

This drill with your head against the wall keeps the forward-bend position correct as you swing. The key is to make a three-quarter swing motion while your head stays touching the wall.

HEAD STAYS IN CONTACT

Place yourself in a good golf athletic position and bend forward at the waist so your head touches the wall.

Make a backswing pivot with your head. Your head should remain touching the wall.

Pivot to the follow-through position as you keep your head touching the wall.

RIGHT PASSES LEFT WALL DRILL

This drill helps limit the amount of hip slide you can have on the downswing. It is a four-step drill.

SET UP

Place your left foot up against the wall. Place yourself in a good golf athletic position. Cross your arms and rest them on the opposite shoulder.

BACKSWING TURN

Turn to a good backswing position. Do not allow your hips to touch the wall.

DOWNSWING

As the weight transfers, the left leg straightens but does not touch the wall. Notice how the weight is shifting toward the target.

FOLLOW-THROUGH

The left hip passes the wall. The right shoulder touches the wall.

PROBLEM POSITIONS

These photos illustrate some problems the drill will detect. The left hip has slid into the wall, and as a result the correct follow-through position cannot be achieved.

RIGHT SIDE SHAFT DRILL

These drills help you feel what the right side of the body should be doing during the swing. I'm using an old golf shaft, but a dowel pushed into the ground will work just as well.

SET UP

Place the shaft into the ground outside the right foot so that it goes in front of the right knee cap. You want to develop the sense that everything can turn around the right shin on the backswing.

ADDRESS

With the shaft in the ground, put yourself in a good golf athletic position at address. The shaft should be by the kneecap and alongside the right shin.

BACKSWING

Make a backswing turn. The shaft will touch the right knee and shin, acting as a governor, to let you know they can go no farther to the right. The body has turned around them to the top of the backswing with only the knee making a very slight movement to the right.

FOLLOW-THROUGH

The shaft is left behind as the downswing goes to the follow-through position. This has clearly been a swing with excellent weight shift and without wasted motions.

INSIDE RIGHT FOOT DRILL

As the body turns on the backswing, this drill provides a way to keep the weight on the inside of the right foot so you don't sway to the outside.

Place the shaft on the ground under the outside front of the right foot.

ADDRESS

Begin with a good golf athletic position with the arms crossed and hands resting on the opposite shoulders.

BACKSWING

As you coil up on the backswing, notice how the right foot is still the focus point for the weight. It stays under the inside of the foot.

FOLLOW-THROUGH

As the swing progresses to follow-through, the right foot pivots and finishes on the toe.

BREAKING OUT
WORK LIST FOR SUCCESS

1. Learn to pivot like a pro at home.

2. Practicing in front of the mirror can accelerate your learning experience.

3. Actually do the drills; don't just read about them.

4. Videotaping the drills will allow you to see your progress.

5. Whenever something starts to go wrong in your swing, do these drills to get back on track.

Pros' Pivot Drills

13

PROS' ARM
SWING

Sergio Garcia's swing changes are clearly evident when comparing old Sergio (red) with new Sergio (silver) in the photo at left. In this TaylorMade MATT system computer snapshot of both versions of his swing, the older one even had a bit of chicken wing in it as well.

What he has improved is the left arm straightening after impact. While his wrist was flat, the elbow used to be bent but now is straight. Just past this position both arms will be straight in the silver version. That is the goal for improving your game, too. The right arm and wrist bends during the swing, but past impact the wrist stays bent while the right arm straightens.

The body may do all the work as far as moving the arms, the way a motor moves the blades of a helicopter. But the arms aren't just along for the ride. They are responsible for transferring the energy the body creates down through the hands, the club shaft and then into the ball.

One of golf's major fundamentals involves the arms. To learn to straighten the right arm without straightening the right wrist is one of the biggest things poor golfers just do not do. They tend to flip the right wrist around instead of keeping it bent.

Remember that at impact you need to have a flat left wrist and a bent right wrist. You need to straighten the right arm without straightening the right wrist. The drills in this chapter will help support that effort.

RIGHT HAND MOTION

At this stage it is important to understand exactly what role both hands play. For demonstration purposes and without a club, let's look at some shorter swings and the right hand's role in them. Putting and chipping are in that category.

RIGHT HAND: PUTTING

As I go from address (left) throughout the stroke notice how the bend in my right wrist is maintained (center). Even as the right arm straightens past simulated impact (right), the bend is still intact.

RIGHT HAND: CHIPPING

As the right arm goes back notice the angle formed at the wrist with the hand. This is the angle we dealt with earlier in the book; this is the pros' angle. You will learn it and use it to improve your game.

QUICK QUIZ

What's wrong in this photo? The angle in the right wrist is gone.

PUNCH

Here is a good way to think of the right arm. It delivers a knockout punch to the ball.

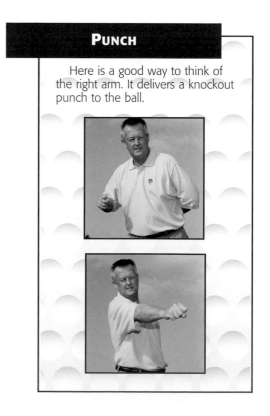

LEFT HAND MOTION

Again for demonstration proposes and without a club, let's take a look at the left arm in short swing situations. It must have a close relationship with the body, so I'm inserting a towel between my arm and chest and must hold it in this position.

To show the close relationship between body and left arm, I insert a towel between them.

During the putting stroke, the towel must stay in place.

DISCONNECT

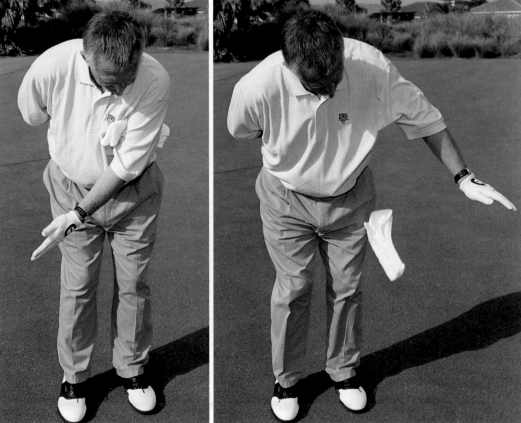

If the left arm incorrectly moves independently away from the body, the towel falls. But let's look at another aspect of this. Is the left arm straight in this past-impact position? No it's not. Is the wrist straight? No, it's bent. Avoid this disconnect at all costs.

LEARN THE MOTION

Now it's your turn. After seeing the demonstration as to the correct motion of both arms and wrists, try this drill that will help you feel exactly how to swing and maintain the pros' angles.

SET BOTH WRIST ANGLES

Cross your wrists in front of you, bend the right wrist back, place the left hand against the bend so the wrist stays flat, and, with a little pressure, keep them together during the practice swing, which is one way to make sure the right wrist stays bent and the left wrist stays flat.

GOOD SEQUENCE

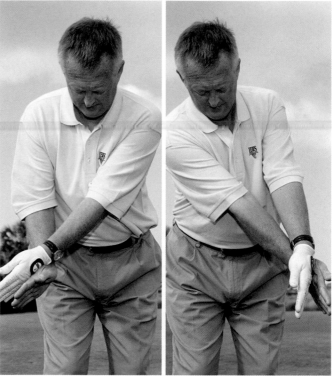

Swing your arms slightly back and forth. Keep the straight left wrist and bent right wrist throughout. Sense what this feels like. It is important to program this feeling.

FRED FUNK PAST IMPACT

Fred Funk ranks No. 1 in driving accuracy on the PGA TOUR. Look at his past-impact position thanks to the TaylorMade MATT system. Both arms are straight. They have delivered the power the body created. Any bend or wrist flip leaks away that power.

This is not a simulation of Fred's swing. He wore specialized clothing and swung a club fitted with computer sensors, which special cameras with the computer converted to this image.

EXTEND THE SWING

This drill extends the swing back and through. The angles will stay the same, but to achieve this position, practice is needed.

SET THE ANGLE

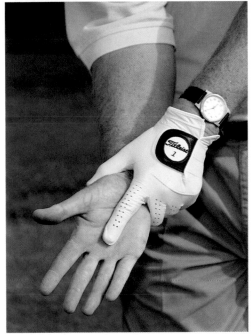

Place the index finger of the left hand against the palm of the right hand. Clasp the right hand with the thumb and other fingers of the left hand. The bend in the right wrist should be formed, and grasping it will maintain it throughout this practice-swing drill.

ADDRESS

Start with a good golf athletic position with your hands in front. Notice the bend in the right wrist. Remember, if we secured a hinge to the right wrist it would be on the back of the wrist so it could only bend.

PITCHING MOTION

During the pitching motion, the right arm can bend on the backswing. Past impact, the arm straightens. The right wrist bend remains constant throughout this pitch. Practice this drill several times to program the feel.

How Best to Learn the Game

Instead of jumping right into the full swing, you stand a better chance of developing a pro-type swing if you start small and work your way up. That is why we began with putting examples and then moved to pitching and chipping. The longer the swing, the more bend in the right elbow, but the past-impact position is the same. You must straighten both arms but retain the flat left wrist and bent right wrist. Now we can begin with some longer swings, working on this same basic fundamental.

Three-quarter Swing Basketball Drill

Using a two-tone basketball clearly demonstrates what the arms should be doing in your golf swing. You can do this in front of a mirror at home because you want to see two different colors, depending on the swing position. The goal is to make sure you get some depth to the arm swing.

Two-Tone Color Setup

At simulated address, you can see the two colors of the ball equally divided in front of me.

Reverse Colors

Notice the reversal of the ball colors at both the top of the backswing and the follow-through.

Two-Tone Ball with a Club

Now it is time to put a club in the swing. This time I have put a smaller two-tone ball between my arms. As I swing you should see only one color on the backswing and the other color on the follow-through.

See Colors Separately

The key here is that you see blue on the backswing and green on the follow-through.

Follow-through

It would have been disastrous if you had seen both colors on the side on the follow-through, as that would have indicated poor arm action. Notice how I combined a correct body pivot with the wrist positions to arrive at this good position.

DEPTH TO THE ARMS

This great drill will help you correctly follow a path on the backswing and also on the follow-through. It is really the 45-degree-to-45-degree drill because all you have to do is have your arms parallel to the clubs on the ground to be in a good position.

SETTING UP

Start with a long PVC pipe or broomstick as the target line. Place one club perpendicular to the line (center club), which is 90 degrees. Using that club as a guide, place two clubs at an angle that is either half or 45 degrees.

SETTING UP CHECK

When you remove the perpendicular 90-degree club your instant practice station should look like this.

PARALLEL ARM BACKSWING

When you rotate and bring the club back, your left arm should be close to parallel with the backswing club on the ground.

PARALLEL ARM FORWARD SWING

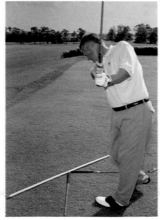

As you rotate and bring the club to this past-impact position, the right arm should be close to parallel to the other club on the ground.

HAND DRILLS

The hands have to be trained to do what is required of them during the swing. The wrist angles are important. With these two drills without using a club, you can easily master where the hands are in the swing and the feeling for those positions.

RIGHT HAND DRILL

Start with only your right hand, and simply point your thumb to your opposite shoulder as you go to the top of the backswing and then rotate to follow-through. Think, "Thumb's to the left, thumb's to the right."

SETUP

Begin with only your right hand extended in front.

TOP OF BACKSWING

At the top of the backswing, the right thumb should be pointed to the top right shoulder.

FOLLOW-THROUGH

On the follow-through, the right thumb should be pointed to the left shoulder.

BOTH HANDS DRILL

SETUP

This is the same type of drill as the previous one, but this time use both hands. Begin with both hands simulating a grip in front of your body.

BACKSWING

When you rotate to the top of the backswing, your thumbs should both be pointed toward the right shoulder.

FOLLOW-THROUGH

At the follow-through position, verify your thumbs are now pointing to the left shoulder.

LEVEL ELBOW DRILL

With this drill you can work on getting your elbows as level as Tom's are. I'm using a bar that has a piece of webbing attached to both ends. It is very simple to make even with a wood strip. You don't have to have exactly what I'm using to do these drills. Be creative and innovative.

LEVEL BAR

With the bar attached to both arms at the address position, I swing back to near the top of my backswing. Notice the bar is parallel to the ground, indicating the elbows are level.

The left elbow also needs training after impact. You have heard of the dreaded chicken wing, where the elbow pops out past impact. This drill will stop that from ever happening in your swing.

CHICKEN WING

Avoid this position where the elbow pops out, looking like a chicken wing past impact.

ELBOW LOCK

To hold the elbow in place, insert your right hand between your chest and left elbow. Setting the right wrist bend, press it up against the back of the left elbow.

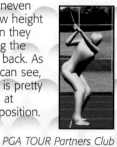
LEFT ELBOW IN PLACE

This sequence shows how the elbow is kept in position so it does not pop out like a chicken wing past impact.

BOX DRILL

You don't need a box for this drill. Your right upper arm, right forearm and the shaft should make up three sides of the box at the correct top of the backswing.

THREE SIDES OF THE BOX

At the top of the backswing notice how my right upper arm #1 joins with my forearm #2 and the shaft #3 to form three sides of a box.

UN-BOX IT

Once you have the box at the top you now must straighten out the sides as I have done here. Notice how the bend in the right wrist is maintained even as the arm straightens past the impact position.

RIGHT ELBOW DRILL

Many high-handicap players have a wandering right elbow that invades space where it should not be. This can be eliminated by training it to stay in its own designated area during the swing.

ELBOW #1 DRILL

SETTING UP

Begin with a good athletic golf address posture position. Never shirk on posture. Place the back of the left hand on the outside of the right elbow.

BACKSWING

With the left hand as an elbow side motion limiter, rotate to the top of the backswing position. Notice the bend in the right wrist at the top of the backswing. This keeps the right elbow from getting too far behind your body.

FOLLOW-THROUGH

With the left hand still pressed against the right elbow, rotate to the follow-through position. Notice the bend in the right wrist at the finish.

COMPARE THESE LOOKS

This is a good illustration of what a world-class player and a poor player would look like if they took their right hands off the club at the moment the club was descending.

DESCENDING CLUB

The club is descending on the path toward the ball. If we stopped the action abruptly and removed the right hands from the grip, the next two photos would show the difference between a pro and poor player.

PRO

The right arm would spring out as a result of pushing on the downswing.

AVERAGE PLAYER

The right arm would come closer to the body because this player was pulling his hands slightly toward his body on the downswing.

BREAKING OUT
WORK LIST FOR SUCCESS

1. Work on correct arm motion, starting with small swings.

2. Stretch that out to a full swing with specific drills to keep you on the arc.

3. Always make sure your posture is correct before doing any drill. Never practice mistakes.

4. A mirror at home can help you, even with arm motions. You're doing stop-action positions to verify correctness.

5. Don't try to work on too much at any one time. Master key areas before moving on to the next, especially if you are working at home on this facet of your game.

14 DEVELOP A PRO'S HANDS AND WRISTS

Darren Clarke has been a successful player on both the European Tour and PGA TOUR. He recognizes that his hands are the connection to the club. Hands have a massive influence on how the clubface is presented to the ball. In the TaylorMade MATT system computer-generated photo (at left) of Darren at impact, you can see the clubface is square to his target line. That was the work of his left hand.

The body has the job to create energy, the arms to transfer it and the hands to sense and monitor both the clubhead and clubface. You can train your hands. The left wrist must be flat just after impact because that controls the clubface. The right wrist must be bent back slightly at and just after impact. This is what creates the thump, the wallop. These are the pros' moves.

The reason that less-proficient golfers can't achieve the wallop at impact is because they use their wrists incorrectly. They are trying to square the clubface with their right hand, which causes a problem, because that is the job of the left hand. The left hand should square up the clubface, not the right hand. If that doesn't occur, then nothing good will happen.

The drills in this chapter will help your hands and wrists behave as they should. The opening drills help you sense what the back of the left hand does with the goal of getting the clubface squared at impact to make the ball go straight.

BACK OF THE LEFT HAND

Here is a great way to illustrate that whatever the back of the left hand does, the clubface must do too. Poke a rubber driving range practice tee through the back of an old glove. Now the back of my left hand can do some pointing to illustrate exactly what that means to the golf swing.

POINTING TO PROGRESS

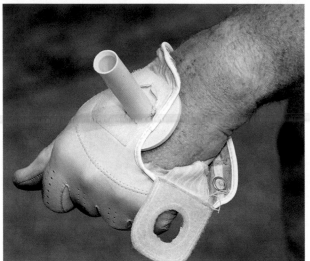

I inserted a practice range rubber tee through the back of an old glove to illustrate the connection between the back of the left hand and the clubface.

CHALK TALK

BACK OF YOUR HAND:

What I have done with the driving range tee and the glove should become a positive mental image for you. Think that you have a tee on the back of your glove and that when your wrist is flat at impact and beyond, that the ball will be going in the direction the back of the hand is pointed.

If the back of the left hand is a right angle to the target line, the ball will go straight. But if the back of the hand is pointed either to the left or to the right, the ball has no other option than to go in the direction the back of the hand was pointed at impact.

CLUBFACE AND THE LEFT HAND

In the next three photos I gripped down the shaft so that my left hand is right above the clubface. As I turn the wrist in various directions, notice how the clubface points exactly where the back of my left hand is pointing.

The clubface points exactly where the back of the left hand is pointing.

NORMAL GRIP

Gripping the club normally, once again it is clear that wherever the back of the left hand points, the clubface has no other option but to point in the same direction. The most important lesson to learn from these photos is that you want the back of the left hand and clubface to point straight down a line parallel to the target at impact.

The easiest way to accomplish this is with a flat left wrist. There are no shortcuts, and physics does not lie. You have but one option, and a wrist that is not flat at impact may be the biggest culprit in what has been stopping your improvement.

BACK OF LEFT HAND DICTATES

Just as it did when I gripped down the shaft, the clubface points exactly in the same direction as the back of the left hand.

HAND-CLUB CONNECTIONS

What the heel of your hand does, the heel of the club does. What the left thumb does the toe of the club does. So when less-proficient golfers move the wrist back and forth, the toe does not necessarily go over the heel as it must.

If you are slicing, the heel of your hand is coming through the ball first. If you are hooking, then the toe is coming through first. Each golfer has his or her problems.

CLUB MOUNTED ON THE LEFT HAND

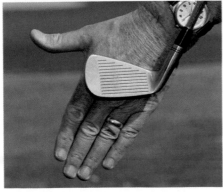

If you could mount a club on the back of the left hand; the toe would be the left thumb, and the heel of your hand would be the heel of the club.

MOUNTED CLUBFACE

I have drawn the clubface on the back of my hand to demonstrate that what the back of the hand does, the clubface must also do.

BALL DIRECTION DRILLS

This drill will be done three ways to improve direction and create the pro's thump and wallop at impact.

LEFT HAND DRILL

Place your right hand behind your back. With the correct left grip, place the club behind the ball. Your feet should be ahead about two feet. Walk forward, allowing the clubface to stay in contact rolling the ball.

RIGHT HAND DRILL

Place your left hand behind your back. With the correct right-hand grip, place the club behind the ball. Your feet should be ahead. Walk forward, allowing the clubface to stay in contact rolling the ball.

BOTH HANDS DRILL

Grip the club with both hands. With your feet ahead, let the clubface roll the ball along the ground as you walk forward. The clubface is controlling the ball's direction. You should feel the left hand controlling the clubface, and you should feel the right hand supplying the power to roll the ball.

THE BIG THUMP

This is an impact drill. With the clubface position taken care of by the left wrist, the right hand needs to apply the power generated from the body down through the arms and into the club. If you have two tennis rackets at home with their covers on, you can duplicate the pro's thump.

ADDRESS

Set up as if you had a ball in front of you. Hold the two rackets and line them up just to the left of your left armpit. Remember: The lowest point of the swing is the left armpit and you want the ball just before it.

DOWNSWING

Swing the racket back toward the stationary racket. The right wrist is still bent. You can sense the power coming toward the ball. There is very little body motion; this is about bending and straightening the right arm.

IMPACT

The racket in the right hand thumps into the stationary left-hand racket. The right arm straightens. The right wrist retains some bend angle. This transferred the power from one racket to the other with a thump, just as the clubhead will transfer the energy to the ball with a thump.

QUICK QUIZ

Which of the three photos would you want for your left wrist and hand position at impact? It's obviously #1. Which photo has the flat left wrist? #1 again! Get the picture? You need a flat left wrist at impact to improve your game significantly.

1   **2**   **3**

Develop a
Pro's
Hands
and Wrists

LEFT WRIST COCK AND UNCOCK DRILL

Find a coat hanger at home that you can attach or tape to a shaft. A plastic hanger works best because the hook must stay in contact with your forearm when the wrist cocks correctly.

SETTING UP

With a coat hanger attached to the club so that the hook points outward, grip the club with just your left hand.

LEFT WRIST COCK

On the backswing the left wrist is cocked. If it had a hinge, the hinge would be on top so the wrist can only move up and down, never side to side. The wrist does rotate slightly due to the arm motion. As you can see, the hook now rests up against the forearm.

DOWNSWING UNCOCKING

This photo sequence shows how the left wrist stays cocked and then begins to uncock as the club reaches a parallel-to-the-ground position.

IMPACT

The left wrist has uncocked. The left wrist is flat. The shaft tilts forward. Note the steel rod relationship between the left arm, wrist and shaft is obvious. This is a pro's position that you can make part of your game.

PAST IMPACT

Past impact, the left arm remains straight and the wrist remains flat.

FOLLOW THROUGH

At follow-through, the hook returns to rest against the left forearm.

THE GOOD AND THE BAD

The final photos show what you want to look like and don't want to look like at impact. Using the hanger as a guide, the "good" would be a good position to practice in front of a mirror at home.

GOOD IMPACT

BAD IMPACT

Your left wrist is flat at impact. Your right wrist is bent at impact. The shaft is tilted forward. Your hands are ahead of the clubhead. The clubface is correctly de-lofted. A flat left wrist starts the ball out straight.

Your left wrist is bent at impact. Your right wrist is straight at impact. The shaft is tilted backward. The clubface loft increased. This is a bad result common to people not reading this book.

BREAKING OUT
WORK LIST FOR SUCCESS

1. Start by understanding what each hand must do during the swing.

2. If you can poke a tee, even a wooden one, through an old glove, grip down by the clubface with your left hand. Point the back of the hand in different directions and see how the clubface follows.

3. Train the left wrist and hand with the drills before moving on. Some can be done at home because you are not hitting balls.

4. Work on a good impact position at home in front of the mirror.

5. Do the thump drill to develop the power phase.

15 PUTTING A PRO'S SWING TOGETHER

Throughout the book you have learned all phases of a pro's swing. Learning how to grip the club, position the ball, hinge the wrists, pivot the body, transfer power from the arms and control the hands has all led up to this chapter on how to put everything together.

The best way to show this interaction is the swing plane. Sergio Garcia's swing plane—the backswing and transition phase—was produced from an actual swing by the TaylorMade MATT system. It provides a good mental image of the swing arc the club follows back and on its return to the ball.

The clubface positions change, but not as a result of manipulation. They change as a function of rotation. I will use a plane board for the demonstration, then will provide some drills for you to work with to put your swing together like a pro.

ON-PLANE CHECKPOINTS

You can't play this game very well unless you understand swing plane. Instead of looking at what you think is a big circle, let's be clever and have some checkpoints along the way.

If you know what to do at the checkpoints, the entire plane falls into line. All that you have learned in this book plays a role, and if you do the drills perfectly your plane will be perfect as well.

When we talk about the club being on plane, we really mean the shaft. We are not just interested in the clubhead. This is why in our next two drills, I will do one with just a shaft and the other with a hockey stick to demonstrate what the clubhead is doing at the checkpoints.

A Dozen Checkpoints

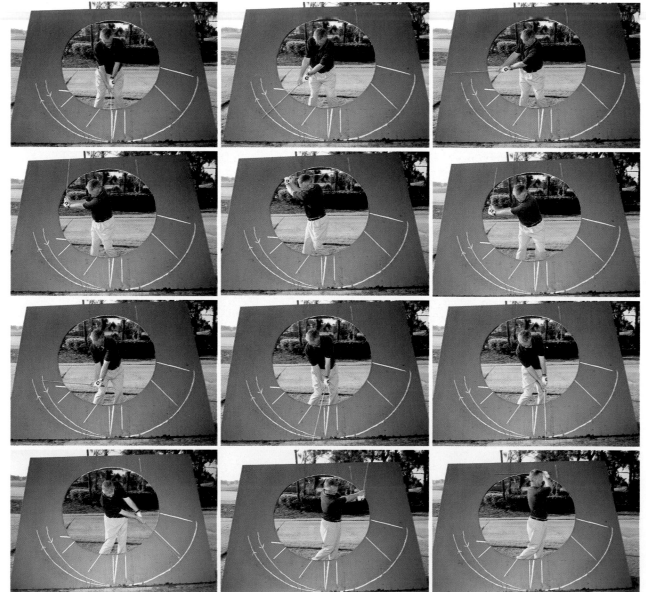

As you look at these checkpoints along the swing plane, concentrate on the various angles of the wrists, especially when the left wrist cocks and uncocks. You will find some easy-to-do swing-plane drills that will help accomplish all of this, but for now just familiarize yourself with the concept of the plane.

Look at the swing plane and how a clubhead would react to the wrist, arm and hand positions at the various checkpoints. A hockey stick plays the role of the clubhead to emphasize how the face of the club would react to the wrist hinge angles during the swing plane.

CHALK TALK

TWO RULES FOR THE SWING PLANE WHEN HITTING A STRAIGHT SHOT:

Rule # 1: Whichever end of the club could point to the target line should point to the target line.

Rule #2: If either end of the club is pointing at the target line or is parallel to the target line.

BACKSWING AND DOWNSWING:
SAME PLANE BUT DIFFERENT CLUBHEAD TRACK

Ideally your takeaway and the movement back into the ball would be on the same plane. But that does not mean the club goes up and down in the same place. The arrows on the swing-plane board illustrate the difference.

OUTSIDE/UP—INSIDE/DOWN

The outside arrows are the path the clubhead takes going back. The inner arrows are the path it takes on the return to the ball.

BACKSWING/OUTSIDE ARC

The clubhead follows the outside arrows as the body rotation and arms bring the clubhead back from the ball.

DOWNSWING/INSIDE ARC

The clubhead follows the inside arrows on the way down to the ball. Every good player has a downswing that is sharp, narrower or steeper than the backswing. You want to keep backswing and downswing on the same plane going back and down but not in the same place.

Putting a Pro's Swing Together

WHY THE CLUB FOLLOWS INSIDE ARC ON DOWNSWING

If the club goes back on one arc, why doesn't it return in the same place on the way down? The answer: the little shift of weight to the front foot as the downswing begins. The wrists are relaxed as you start down. You are not forcing the club with your hands from the top down.

INSIDE ARC

My slight weight shift forward is one reason the club follows an inside arc instead of the outside arc on which it went back. The shaft is on the same plane but the clubhead is at different places.

CHALK TALK

SOME NONSENSE AND RUBBISH:

You hear less-knowledgeable golfers talk about the inside loop and that you drop the club to the inside loop. That is nonsense! You want the club to come down on the same plane it went back, but the clubhead is not in the same place. Remember when we talk about swing plane it refers to the shaft being on plane.

Those who think they want a wider swing arc coming into the ball would think the arcs seen here are just the opposite. That is rubbish! You can't manufacture these positions. They are the result of correct wrist hinge angles, posture, alignment and body pivot with arm swing. The clubhead will follow or not follow the inside arc naturally, not because you want it to. It all depends on your fundamentals.

SWING PLANE SELF-TEST

This is a good drill that will help you check your swing plane. You can do it in the backyard before going to the range. It's a do-it-yourself swing-plane trainer.

CONSTRUCT SWING TRAINER

Use a piece of string or rope that is about 50-inches long. I taped it, at eye height, to a piece of PVC pipe and base that is easy to make yourself. Or you could tape the string to a wall. I also taped together a loop at the end of the string.

STRING SHOULD STAY TIGHT

As I do the drill, if my swing plane is correct, the string will stay tight.

ADDRESS

Slip the loop over the grip and hold it in place as you grip the club. The string should be tight.

BACKSWING TIGHT

As you swing the club back, if all is okay with your swing plane the rope will stay tight.

DOWNSWING TIGHT

Returning back along the same plane will keep the rope tight.

HITTING AREA TIGHT

From impact to past impact, the string remains tight as the shaft is still on the correct swing plane. Notice how my arms straightened after impact, which kept the rope tight. I'm hitting a ball, but in your backyard you can use a whiffle golf ball or do the drill with a tee.

FAIL POSITIONS

Your swing may have looked like this at any one of these positions. You can't fool the swing trainer. When the rope goes loose, the swing trainer immediately detects that you are off plane.

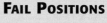

PLANE TRAINING DRILL

Making repetitive swings while keeping your upper arms under the angled shafts provides an excellent arm plane method for learning the correct path of the swing plane. I have used six old shafts and placed three together for each side of the swing.

ADDRESS

SWING

The shaft poles I have constructed are angled into the ground so they bisect my right and left shoulders when I address the ball. I have also secured a target line to the ground. Note that I'm addressing a tee where the ball would normally be.

Swing the club keeping your upper arms under the shafts as you swing. The left upper arm stays under the shaft on the backswing. As you swing down and through, the right upper arm stays under the shaft on the follow-through.

CUSHION COMFORT

These pads are called the "Insider" and are typically used to help keep golfers from coming over the top on the downswing. Using two of them together works like bookends keeping the swing on a nice straight plane. I set the right one just outside the right shoulder at about 45 degrees. The left one is reversed, just outside the left shoulder at about 45 degrees. Like the string drill this is not for hitting golf balls, but it definitely gives you a good path for the hands to travel on.

DOWNSWING

The hands stay under the pads as you swing to the top of the backswing and then down toward the hitting area. The arms swing back along the chest at about 45 degrees to the target line, which is why the pads were set at that angle.

PAST IMPACT

The hands stay under the pad as the club passes through the hitting area. Just as on the backswing, 45 degrees is the angle to the target line. The hands swing back along the chest.

BOLSTER YOUR PLANE

This drill provides the slot to swing through in the hitting area. I had some bolsters made that were on an angle. Vijay Singh does a similar drill with shafts on the ground and sets them up for a very narrow hitting area.

FOLLOW THE PATH

Swinging through the cushions provides a swing plane path to follow through the hitting area. I angled the cushions so they are parallel to my shaft.

TRACER SWING TEST

This training device gives you a path to swing through. The pegs indicate if your club strayed off the swing plane in the hitting area. I added a bolster and placed it by the outside of the path as the club enters.

PASSED

This swing stayed on plane and did not cause any of the indicator pegs to move.

FAIL: SLICE PATH

The bolster was hit as the club swung into the hitting area from outside in. The farthest inside peg was moved by the club slicing through on an outside-in path.

FAIL: HOOK PATH

The two farthest outside pegs were moved because the club came from too inside the path and was swinging inside to outside.

FAIL: TOE HIT

This was a toe hit because the Swing Tracer shows the club veered to the inside and moved the two farthest inside pegs.

SHOULDER SWING DRILL

LIMIT SWAY

One problem some golfers have is swinging the club too far back. This drill limits the amount of backswing. The key is the right arm must stop the swing before it touches the noodle.

This drill keeps my body from swaying. You could also use two waist-high cardboard boxes and place them in a similar position as the foam pieces sticking out from this device. The key is to stay corralled.

PROBLEM

The hands have reached a 12 o'clock position, which is too far. To be safe you have to get home before 12.

SETTING UP

I placed a foam noodle on a microphone stand just above my shoulder height.

SLIDE LIMITS

GOOD STOPPING POINT: 10 O'CLOCK

This is a good place to stop the backswing. The hands are in a 10 o'clock position and the arms are not touching the noodle.

When is there too much lower body sliding? This drill stops it by letting me know when I've exceeded the limit. Address the ball and make a complete swing. A good body pivot would prevent you from running into the foam reminders. On the downswing, when the weight transfers to the target side of the body, you still must sway no farther than over your left leg.

DOWEL DRILL

Using two long dowels will help you learn the swing plane. We start with an easily visible horizontal plane, move it down to 45 degrees and then finish with the golf swing plane.

HORIZONTAL PLANE

It's easy to visualize a plane when it is horizontal. Start with your hands horizontal in front of you and swing only the right dowel back. Return the right dowel to meet the left one.

45-DEGREE SWING PLANE

At 45 degrees the brain can easily recognize the circular motion of the swing. Start with your hands at about a 45-degree angle to the ground and swing only the right dowel back and then return the right dowel to meet the left one.

SWING PLANE

With the brain freshly programmed for the concept of swinging on a plane, do this: Place both dowels so they touch the ground on the angle of a golf shaft. Without any body motion swing the right dowel back on the swing plane. Return the right dowel to the left dowel down along the plane. Repeat several times. This is also a good drill to do on the range or during a round, but substitute two clubs for the dowels.

AIM SWING PLANE TO TARGET

In a nutshell, these photos show how important it is to aim your swing plane to the target if you want to hit a straight shot. I'm using a swing plane aid to show swing direction and a piece of rope that will serve as the target line.

STRAIGHT SHOT SWING PLANE

This swing plane allows me to hit shots straight down the target line.

LEFT SWING PLANE

This swing plane is definitely aimed to the left of the target line, which is where the ball will start off.

RIGHT SWING PLANE

This swing plane is aimed right of the target line, the direction the ball will go if this is your swing plane.

BREAKING OUT
WORK LIST FOR SUCCESS

1. Build a swing plane practice station with PVC poles, or use string taped to a wall.

2. Understand the role of various checkpoints in the swing plane by looking at the three sequence photo groups (on pages 124 and 125).

3. Understand that working on the positions you have learned throughout the book will keep you on plane, not trying to manipulate yourself into each position.

4. Be inventive and find household objects to simulate some of the unique training aids shown here. Foam noodles and dowels can be used for many of these drills.

5. Find the drills that work best for you and learn how you can adapt them during a round if you feel you are getting off plane.

16 EQUIPMENT THAT WILL HELP YOUR GAME NOW

Real improvement comes from learning how to swing like a pro. Today's cutting-edge equipment, however, is primarily responsible for the quantum leap forward in the increased distance and lower scores players are achieving. If you can hit the ball farther and play wedges into the greens, your scores will go lower! Some players can now reach par-4 holes off the tee.

The old rules of keeping the ball low have been replaced by equipment designed to increase launch angles and reducing ball spin rotation. The net results are a longer hang time in the air and, because the ball doesn't spin as much, greater distance on the carry.

Manufacturers like TaylorMade spend considerable time and money developing a range of new products for average golfers. Recreational golfers are the core market for equipment companies. Instead of using focus groups, they count on their staff of PGA TOUR players to provide product feedback.

The goal of equipment today is to get golfers custom fit for clubs and shafts that can improve their game in its present state. Compensation for the swing problems individual golfers face is easier than changing golfer's techniques. Customized adjustments in clubhead weighting, matching a shaft to swing speeds, along with the advances in a new range of balls, are playing a big role in helping golfers improve while getting more enjoyment from the game.

Before going inside TaylorMade for insight on how this new golf equipment can help your game, we begin with PGA TOUR Partners Club member Lou Rinaldi, who has developed a training aid that helps golfers train themselves as they swing along the actual swing plane.

THE GROOVE

Lou Rinaldi is one of those gifted athletes who excel in any sport they try. He played professional soccer for the New York Cosmos alongside the legendary Pelé. But when it came to golf, the swing plane mystified him.

Lou was an 18 handicap who, like you, wanted to improve. But the swing plane concept had him mixed up. "How do I visualize it? How do I relate to it? I needed to do something to improve. I needed something that would let me see this swing path so I could understand what I needed to make my body do."

Based on his training as an engineer, Rinaldi arduously researched the golf swing. He painstakingly traced the path of the club inch by inch from impact back to where the club approached the ground. Then he mapped out the path the club had to take past impact.

Lou traced this route onto a tin sheet and then cut out the swing path. Using this template for the golf swing, Lou worked on his swing and within a year dropped from an 18 to a 3 handicap and won the club championship at Trump National. Lou has since gone on to become one of the most dominant players in the very competitive New York Metropolitan tri-state area, winning numerous tournaments.

From that same tin template, Lou had molds created. Then he produced an impact-proof plastic version, a product he calls THE GROOVE. It also has visual training aids that help golfers practice by swinging along the swing path, which, thanks to Lou Rinaldi, they can now see.

THE GROOVE

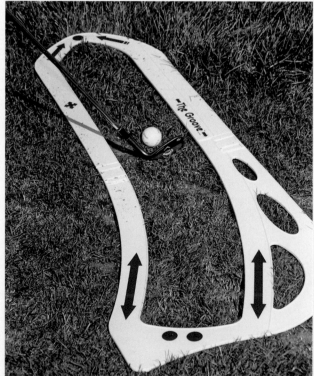

THE GROOVE is a swing training aid that allows golfers to practice swinging along the correct swing plane, both indoors and on the range. As an added benefit, you can hit off real grass with every club from driver through wedge.

ON THE PRACTICE TEE

PGA TOUR Partners Club member Lou Rinaldi on the practice tee as fellow members at Trump National practice using THE GROOVE, the training aid he developed.

HOW IT WORKS

Lou coaches a fellow Trump National member's son. He explains, and can visually show, the swing path to take the club back and then follow toward impact with the ball.

INSTANT SATISFACTION

Lou watches as the young golfer swings back following the path of THE GROOVE, which automatically puts his club on the correct swing plane. At impact and then continuing past impact, the club follows the correct path.

THE GOLF BALL

How do pros select their balls and what do they recommend? Pros don't begin, as you might have thought, in trying to find the ball that gets them the longest distance off the tee. They start alongside the green to find the ball that reacts best to their short game.

The reason has everything to do with saving strokes. It is more important to have a ball that performs its best in the scoring zone. A ball that has feel and characteristics that best enhance your approach shots, short game and putting should be your choice. Pros start with the ball and then select the club specs to match it.

The engine of the ball is its core, and companies like TaylorMade have their own proprietary design concepts for balls. Mike Ferris, senior marketing director for TaylorMade golf balls, explains that in the company's new range of TP balls, basic design characteristics exist for each. "We spent three years designing these new balls," says Ferris. "We wanted to create a yardage-enhancing launch condition coupled with a Tour-quality spin that yielded control and feel."

The TP Red has a thicker core and thinner mantle than the TP Black. What does that translate into as far as performance?

• The TP Black will have a higher launch angle and longer hang time than the TP Red.

• The TP Red will have a softer sound and feel with more of a Tour launch angle. Like the TP Black, it also provides maximum distance.

• If you like a ball with more feel around the greens, choose the TP Red.

• If you need to hit the ball higher to gain distance with low ball spin, select the TP Black.

The old way of thinking was that if you weren't a very good player, then a harder ball should be your choice. Conversely, if you were a good player you would want a softer ball.

Technology started changing in 1996 when multi-layered balls started coming into play with the advent of the Strata. The major step forward was the groundbreaking Titleist Pro V1. That was the end of the era of wound balls, which coincided with the end of wooden drivers.

Now with multi-layered balls (TaylorMade's three-piece) engineers can literally tune the spin curve by the club used. With the new TP range of balls, golfers can have the same backspin they would have had with a two-piece ball. That same ball also provides a low-spin, high-launch capability.

The new ball technology develops less spin off the driver, without sacrificing spin around the greens. In the past when launch angle and spin rates were unheard of, you probably chose a ball that had the reputation for being long off the tee. Today's balls are engineered to be long off the tee and soft around the greens.

HERE IS WHAT TAYLORMADE DEVELOPED

Ball	Core	Mantle
The TP Red	1.510"	.055"
The TP Black	1.480"	.070"

SELECTING THE RIGHT BALL AND EQUIPMENT

All the manufacturers have found that they need to provide demo days for golfers around the country. In some cases they send vans that are similar to those that follow the PGA TOUR.

The vans are equipped with launch monitors that are set up on the range. Just like the pros do weekly, recreational golfers can try out a variety of clubs and balls to find the best combination.

DEMO DAYS

TaylorMade, like most original equipment manufacturers, travels nationwide setting up demo days at golf courses. Usually they set up a launch monitor that will show exactly what the ball does with each club you hit.

LAUNCH MONITOR

| MAKE PDF | PRINT | |< | < | > | >| | BACK |

Shot Analysis   **Trajectory**   TRACKMAN
PROVIDED BY
ISG A/S

DATE : 14 March 2006
TIME : 10:28:38

WIND :
ALTITUDE : 0yds
TEMPERATURE : 20°C

Player	Club	Ball	Shots
☐ Bertsch	TM		1

LAUNCH						FLIGHT		LANDING			
CLUB SPEED [mph]	BALL SPEED [mph]	SMASH FACTOR []	VERT ANGLE [deg]	HORZ ANGLE [deg]	SPIN [rpm]	MAX HEIGHT [yds]	CARRY [yds]	SIDE [yds]	VERT LAND [deg]	FLIGHT TIME [s]	LAST DATA [yds]
112	160.1	1.44	10.5	2.0	2921	37.3	260.4	1.5L	49.4	7.12	256.4

The data shown on this TrackMan monitor screen shows:112-mph clubhead speed at impact, 160.1-mph ball speed, 10.5-degree launch angle, 2921-rpm ball spin, 712 seconds of hang time, and 260.4 yards of carry.

CLUB SELECTION

The launch monitor helps a knowledgeable clubfitter find the correct clubhead, weighting and shaft for each golfer's individual swing. PGA TOUR professionals have the game most recreational players would dream of having. Pros are eager to help you improve should the opportunity arise to play in a pro-am. Unfortunately, you would find their driver to be of no help whatsoever to their game if they let you hit it.

The pros would experience the same problem if you gave them your driver in an even swap. Their drivers are tuned for their games, just as your driver should be constructed to maximize your game.

Clubhead weighting and shaft flex are the keys to good club selection. If you are serious about your game never buy a club because it looks good. Test a few clubs to see which performs the best for you. Some clubs, like those offered by manufacturers like TaylorMade, offer the ability to adjust the weighting to compensate for swing flaws. The weighting also allows you to change the characteristics of the club as your swing improves.

Drivers are the most expensive club in your bag. If you plan on improving, a good start is to buy a driver with an adjustable weighting system.

MAKING AN EASY ADJUSTMENT

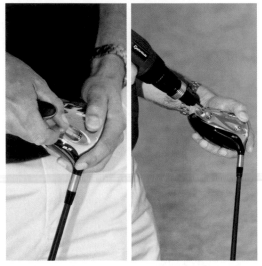

TaylorMade offers a moveable weight system for its drivers. As photographed, a weight is being added to the outside heel. The weight is screwed into place with an automatic screwdriver you may have at home. The benefit is that as your game changes, you can change your driver's characteristics.

A PRO'S WEIGHT DISTRIBUTION

Here is a chart for five TaylorMade staff players and their choices for weighting their R7 425 TP drivers, which have four weighting ports. The numbers are in grams of weight:

HOW WEIGHTING WORKS

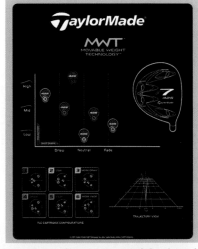

	Front Toe	Back Toe	Back Heel	Front Heel	Ball Flight
Retief Goosen	9	2	2	9	extreme low
Darren Clarke	2	11	11	2	extreme high
Sergio Garcia	8	6	6	8	low
Mike Weir	2	10	10	2	high
Peter Lonard	12	2	12	2	neutral

	Toe		Heel		Ball Flight
	14		2		extreme fade

This diagram shows how changing the weights around the perimeter of the driver's clubhead can correct ball flight. You can adjust the angle of trajectory as well as the off-center deviation. This means that just by adjusting the weights, you can hit the ball higher or lower than your normal swing, correct a fade or draw if that's your problem.

PUTTER TESTING

The TaylorMade MATT system is utilized for helping the pros select the best putter for their individual swings, and no swing is more individual than the putting stroke. Testing can ascertain how different surfaces affect how soon the ball starts rolling after impact.

ON THE SWEET SPOT

The MATT system shows the ball impacting the center of the sweet spot. Data collected from Tour players and amateurs helps the company design and build putters that can improve a golfer's putting by choosing a putter that helps their stroke.

WHICH PUTTER WORKS BEST?

TESTING FACE INSERTS

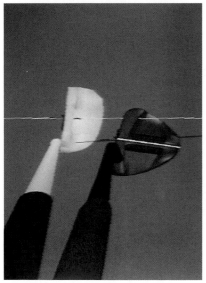

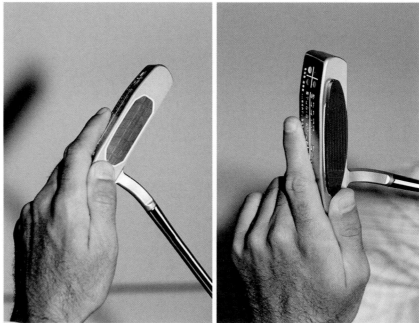

This TaylorMade MATT fitting system screen shows an overlay of two putters being tested. It's easy to see the model on the left is a better choice for the golfer. It's on the target line, while the model on the right does not have a squared face at impact.

As they strive for putting perfection TaylorMade engineers have the ability to test various face inserts to see which inserts promote the ball to roll sooner. Having all this technology available makes your choice easier. However, a putter is such a personal club that it still has to look and feel right for you.

Benoit Vincent is TaylorMade's chief technical officer.

Other factors like clubhead face position at impact and loft angle of the face when it meets the ball are all revealed on the screen. You may have read the putt correctly, but if a putter is not set up properly based on your swing, then the odds for holing the putt are reduced.

Benoit Vincent, TaylorMade's chief technical officer, supervises a vast staff of engineers all dedicated to improving the recreational player's game. His basic philosophy is, "We identify a problem and then it's up to us to solve it." Here are some questions and answers with a man who is on the cutting edge of golf.

Q: *The past few years it seems as if golf has developed a completely new and more technical vocabulary. Do you have a problem in communicating your new technical advances in terms that most golfers can understand?*

A: It's a little problem. In 1990 if you asked U.S. golfers about certain terms, like swingweight, they knew what you meant. It's more challenging today because so much is new. So much of golf research is about numbers and that is hard to get across to golfers—what those numbers mean. I can talk about 5,000 rpm or 7,000 rpm, but the only reference most people have to that is the gauge in their car's instrument panel. Maybe we should write a book titled "Golf by the Numbers."

Q: *So understanding this difficulty in what certain terms mean, how can you help golfers get a better handle on what is being offered and how it can help them?*

A: I did a presentation for our Research and Development staff. Some work on drivers, others on wedges, irons, etc. I was surprised that they didn't understand what the numbers mean for every golf club. They didn't have the big picture until I built a presentation from drivers to putters. We covered all the clubs and spoke in terms of head velocity, ball velocity, launch angle, and how they evolved through a set of clubs.

Dozens and dozens of engineers said this makes sense. This we can understand and how it relates to all the clubs. I gave the same presentation, "How Numbers Evolve," to the PGA Summit, where all the teachers get together, and we made some inroads. People can understand those terms and I think are fascinated by how it affects each club in the set.

So we're not only developing clubs that will help people, we also are developing a new vocabulary that our customers can readily understand. This is important because they will benefit from the technology.

Q: *So you are finding better acceptance of very specific terms to describe the numbers?*

A: We limit our explanation to numbers they've heard on TV, like clubhead velocity, clubhead speed at impact, numbers like that. You'll hear more and more people saying, "I know what my clubhead velocity is." It could be 90 miles per hour or 100 miles per hour, but they have a rough idea and how it compares to a PGA TOUR player.

They know from aids like the Speed Stick, which is plus or minus 10 mph accurate. They also know from launch monitors, which are all over now and measure swing speed. Even on our Web site we ask a few fitting questions, like what club would you play from 150 yards out. We also ask the driving-distance question, which we know people may tend to exaggerate. But from three or four questions we can get a handle on your clubhead velocity.

Q: *What one phrase sums up your philosophy?*

A: Distance with forgiveness. TaylorMade technology is geared toward helping golfers of all abilities drive the ball farther and straighter. If you know you fade and want to draw the ball as your preferred flight pattern, you can change the weighting of the club.

This philosophy of easy-to-hit equipment extends through our complete set of clubs and balls. Custom fitting is important, in fact it's the hottest word in golf today, and we're responsive to that need.

TaylorMade has its own fleet of vans that visit golf courses. They have launch monitors and expert clubfitters. They test you first and are able to build clubs right on the spot. The pros are custom fit for clubs, shafts and balls, and now recreational golfers can have the same attention paid to their games. Matching the right club and shaft swing flex to your individual game will definitely result in improvement.

CUSTOM CLUB FITTING

Throughout this book the TaylorMade MATT fitting system has been utilized as a reference to show the pros at the same positions Martin was discussing. Pros are not the only golfers who can take advantage of this unique way of seeing their swings and learning which club specs best match their ability.

If you're serious about improvement, then consider a set of custom fitted clubs. Visit the TaylorMade Web site, see your local pro or inquire if you have a reputable club fitter in your area. Technology is important and it proves what works best for you. Be as technical as a pro when you choose your clubs.

BREAKING OUT
WORK LIST FOR SUCCESS

1. Understand and then swing along the four feet of the on-the-ground swing plane for a positive approach to practice.

2. To maximize your power and accuracy past impact, swing out instead of around .

3. Select the ball that works best around the greens; that's where most of your strokes come from.

4. Never buy equipment unless you have tested it with your swing on a launch monitor.

5. Launch angle and ball spin rates must be within a specified range to maximize your game. Guesswork is over.

6. Spend some time reading about the new equipment and learning about the benefits before making a purchase. Be informed, know your game and select equipment to improve it. Bargains are no bargain as far as game improvement is concerned.

17 HAS YOUR BODY BEEN HOLDING YOU BACK?

Legendary golfer Walter Hagen had his own unique views of how to take care of his body. When he would show up to the course for his tee time it was after staying up all night carousing at the local nightclubs. When asked why, he answered: "My opponent may have been in his bed but I guarantee he was not sleeping. He was up all night tossing and turning and thinking about this match. If I'm going to be up anyway why not have some fun."

Arnold Palmer once said on the subject of equipment that the most important tool any golfer has is their body. "All the high-tech equipment in the world won't help if your body can't swing the club effectively."

Gary Player was doing stretching exercises when he was in his 20s and his contemporaries would laugh at him. Player went on to win tournaments over four decades, proving that fitness increased his competitive longevity.

Rotational flexibility is vitally important for game improvement. Age may limit some motion, but, unfortunately, most recreational golfers suffer from tight hips and shoulders that limit their flexibility and adversely affect the quality of their golf swings. If the brain can't move a body part, it automatically shifts over to another path compensation—in a vain attempt to accomplish the same goal.

Golf is a game of adapting, but that doesn't work to your advantage if you are trying to compensate for your body. Gina Piazza specializes in helping golfers of all ages improve their flexibility and balance during the swing. With Lou Rinaldi as a willing subject, Gina shows how flexibility, stability and balance can be improved so they can help you break out to lower scores.

PROBLEM: LOSS OF BALANCE—INSTABILITY

Loss of balance causes swaying, sliding and difficulty in generating power in the golf swing. Instability really diminishes your power. In this sequence Lou demonstrates a common problem. His legs are locked, when they need to have a certain amount of flexibility. As a result, his upper body weight leans toward the ball, which creates an unstable platform to swing the club around.

LOOK FAMILIAR?

You've seen this same problem many times while watching others tee off. The locked legs at address limit the hip rotation, which, in turn, limits the backswing. Unable to make the correct turn, this golfer will never be able to break out to lower scores unless he works on his balance.

Gina asked Lou to set up in this position and without telling him was able to push him on his toes with just a slight push with her fingers. This indicates an unstable, unbalanced upper body position problem.

After asking him to return to the address position and knowing he was expecting her to push again, Gina was still able to push him on his toes with both hands. Martin was very clear that a good golf swing is a balanced golf swing, and this common problem needs to be corrected.

LOCATING THE REAL PROBLEM

This problem will not be corrected just by having the golfer bend his knees. The body understands bending, but it's having a problem understanding balance. Here is a test you can give yourself to check your balance.

Begin by standing with your eyes closed. How long can you maintain this position before your body begins to sway? Notice how Lou is beginning to sway to his left. The problem in all of these photos is core stability.

SOLUTION: DEVELOP THE GLUTEAL AND HAMSTRING MUSCLES

Developing the gluteal and hamstring muscles improves balance as a result of reinforced core stability.

CORE STABILITY

Using the large exercise ball, which is readily available, Gina coaches Lou to keep his abdominal muscles pulled inward as he lifts his buttocks off the ground. Key Point: Notice she also has him lying on the ground, with his back flat and with the back of his hands facing down to reinforce good posture at the same time.

To help him strengthen his core, Gina wants Lou to keep the muscles contracted to help keep the ball stable instead of rolling side to side.

ADVANCED CORE

In this exercise Gina has Lou cross his arms over his chest. Not allowing him to use his arms for leverage intensifies the benefits, but it is also more difficult, so you need to work up to it.

With his arms crossed and his muscles contracted, Lou is performing the advanced phase of this exercise.

BENEFIT

Once core stability is improved, a golfer with the unbalanced upper body will be able to get into a good golf athletic position and hold it all through the swing without swaying, leaning or tipping.

BALANCE YOUR SWING

To help you improve even faster while working with this book's drills, it is also important to train the body to feel and understand balance. As we've said throughout the book, "Never practice without feedback."

Balance throughout the swing keeps your body in the correct positions to wallop the ball powerfully at impact. On the other hand, an out-of-balance swing requires all sorts of compensations that compromise your power and accuracy. These balance drills can help.

A number of air-filled, balance-disk training aids are available, and they provide both positive and negative feedback as to how your balance is doing. Both forms of feedback are good in the sense that they let you immediately know whether or not you are in balance. If you're not, stop and start again.

With great appreciation to Donald Trump for allowing these balance drills to be shot at Trump National Golf Club at Briarcliff Manor, Lou and Gina pose with some of the readily available balance training aids.

BACKSWING BALANCE

This drill requires only your back leg and the ground. The key is to stand on one leg. Lou is a lefty so he balances on his left leg. Right-handed golfers will balance on their right legs.

Next Lou rotates to the top of his backswing while remaining balanced on his left leg.

Using half-form Styrofoam rollers, left-hander Lou starts with his normal address position. Primarily self-taught, Lou has his own unique swing. While he may not be textbook at address, his past-impact position is exactly what this book has been emphasizing.

Lou rotates his body back while maintaining his balance throughout the backswing.

Gina places large studded-type disks under the arch of Lou's feet. Both Lou's feet are parallel to the ground, indicating that he is balanced. As he rotates back, Lou's feet remain parallel to the ground, indicating a balanced backswing.

BALANCE DRILL / *POOR BALANCE*   SMALL-DISK BALANCE DRILL

Lou is out of balance. Notice that his toes are pointing down as he rotates back. The air-filled disks placed under his feet immediately signal balance or out of balance.

Except for the size of the disks, this drill is basically the same as the previous one. Place the disks under the balls of your feet rather than your arches. Rotate back to the top of your swing while staying in balance.

CHALK TALK	BACKGROUND ON THE DISKS:	Air disks come in a variety of sizes. As you start to improve your balance and rotation using drills from earlier chapters, you can also fine-tune your balance by switching to smaller air disks that create a balance surface that is harder to stay in. PGA TOUR players also use most of these balance aids when they hit balls on the practice range. Some prefer to hit while wearing socks, saying that it promotes a better sense of the balance points.

STAY IN BALANCE FROM START TO FINISH

This drill utilizes the largest air pillows and a teed ball. The key is to make a full swing so that your back faces the target on the backswing and your chest faces the target on the follow-though.

Swing pace is also important, and if you are not swinging using the pros' technique explained earlier in this book, you will not be in balance. Maintain the angles you have learned, stay in balance, and your scores will start to drop.

FULL SWING BALANCE DRILL

Place balance disks under both feet and address the ball in a balanced position.

Rotate back to the top of the backswing while staying in balance.

Swing down, through impact and to the finish while remaining in balance throughout.

ELIMINATING BODY-CAUSED SWING PROBLEMS

If your current swing resembles a baseball batter instead of a pro golfer, sometimes the reason may be your limited flexibility and lack of ability to reach certain key positions in the golf swing. Gina and Lou start off with an exercise that feels great while it also relaxes the lower back.

LOWER BACK RELAXER

As Lou lies over the ball with his hands on the ground, Gina is instructing him NOT to put his knees on the ground in this starting position.

The next step is move back and forth over the ball. Do not let your knees touch when you return to the original position.

SHOULDER AND BACK STRETCHES

If your golf swing looks like a baseball swing, you may need to do a better job stretching your shoulders and latissimus (back).

SHOULDER AND BACK STRETCH

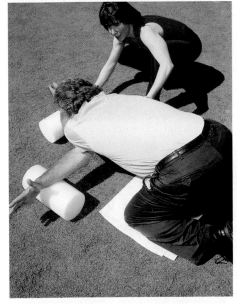

Use two foam rollers for this stretch. First, Gina places Lou's left forearm on the front roller. Lou then places his right forearm across his body on the left roller This is very important: You must sit back on your heels. Move slowly with each arm. Reverse the side roller and change arms to repeat the stretch.

SIDE OF THE BACK STRETCH

As Lou slowly moves his right arm, which is crossed under and now rests on the left roller, he will feel a stretch in the right side of his back. When Lou reverses the arm positions, he will feel a stretch in the left side of his back.

SHOULDER STRETCH

As Lou slowly moves his left outstretched arm, he feels the stretch in his shoulders. Repeat this portion of the drill with the right arm outstretched.

STAY IN CONTROL

Another swing problem that may be attributed to a loss of control can be prevented with the next grouping of exercises. By utilizing different hand positions, different areas will be strengthened for different swing motions.

Weak shoulders may cause loss of control at the top of backswing. The quick fixes will strengthen your shoulders, including the rotator cuff/scapular area.

PALMS BACK EXERCISE

Begin by using a light weight for each hand, but if this is too difficult start without using any weights. The first exercise begins with the palms facing back.

PALMS FACING IN

This exercise begins with the palms facing in. Use only light weights with these exercises, as golf is a sport that requires balanced muscle groups that are rotationally flexible.

IDEAL POSITION

Gina coaches Lou to keep his back flat and abdominal muscles pulled in. As with all exercises, do them slowly to derive maximum benefits.

PULL ARMS UP

Gina makes sure Lou understands that as he pulls his arms up, the back of the forearms should only reach a level T position with the back. These are shoulder strengthening drills.

GOOD BODY POSITION

Lifting the weights is only part of the benefit. To obtain maximum results your body must be in a good position. The back needs to be flat with the neck parallel to the ground, not angled up or down.

ARMS IN LINE

Just as with the first drill in this section the back of your forearms should only reach the level position. Breathe normally so you are relaxed as you do this or any exercise.

PALMS FORWARD EXCERCISE

This exercise mirrors the other two with the only difference being the palm position. While in the other two your palms were facing backward and inward, for this exercise they face the front. Once again, as you lift the light weights, make sure your back begins in a straight and level position. As you lift the weights, your forearms should rise only enough to become level with the back.

LACK OF FLEXIBILITY BETWEEN LOWER AND UPPER BODY

One of the reasons for a reverse spine angle may be a misunderstanding of how you should correctly address the ball, which is a problem with technique. Another possibility may be a lack of flexibility between your upper and lower body. The next group of drills provides a self-test and a way to improve. Coupled with the correct skills and drills in previous chapters, you will find improvement really beginning.

SELF-TEST POSITION

Gina coaches Lou into the correct position to test his spinal rotation flexibility. Lou lies on his back with his knees up and feet on the ground. Lou places his arms above his head and on the ground.

GOOD

In this case Lou is demonstrating good flexibility as his lower body can rotate far enough to the right for his right knee to touch the ground.

POOR

Lou, while keeping his back in the original flat-on-the- ground position, can't touch the ground with his left knee as he rotates his lower body to the left.

STRETCH TO IMPROVE

To help Lou increase his spine rotational flexibility, Gina gently presses his knees downward. This is a gentle push done slowly and with control until resistance is felt; then it's held for about 15 seconds. Gina makes sure that Lou's shoulders remain flat on the ground as he stretches.

HIP FLEXOR FLEXIBILITY

To balance the muscle group that was just stretched, some additional exercises are needed to stretch the hip flexors located in the upper portion of the legs. Once this muscle group is stretched it will be able to enhance a smooth, harmonious balanced swing motion.

Golf flexibility specialists understand that the sport does not require bulking up but does require rotational flexibility. Usually, extra muscle strengthening is needed only to balance the opposing set of muscles if a weakness is detected. This not only creates balanced muscle harmony but also prevents injuries.

HIP FLEXOR STRETCH STEP

The key to this exercise is that the front leg knee never goes over the foot as the stretch progresses. Lou has one knee on the ground. The other knee is up in the air but behind the foot. Best done with a partner; Lou is pressing on Gina's hands before moving into the stretch. This helps him engage his core, which activates the abdominal muscles.

HIP FLEXOR STRETCH STEP

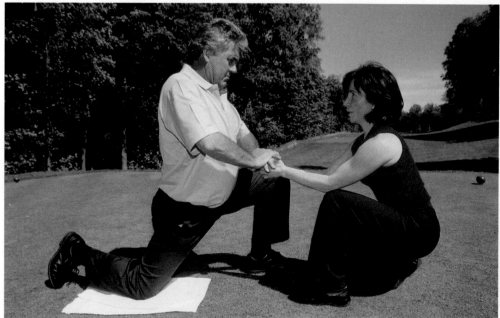

As Lou moves forward on his right knee, the stretch intensifies. Only do this stretch gently until you feel resistance. Hold that position while breathing normally for about 15 seconds. Repeat again, stretching farther. Never allow the up knee to go over the foot. Reverse legs to stretch the other side.

LEGS AND LOWER BODY FLEXIBILITY AND STRENGTH

Hamstrings are the large muscles in the top portion of the back of each leg. Some instructors refer to them as the large muscles that power the swing. This series of self-tests and exercises is designed to test their flexibility and strength and then improve them to help your swing improve.

HAMSTRING STRETCH

Gina helps Lou test the flexibility of his right hamstring. Of course, you do need to test both. Lou is stretched with his back flat on the ground and arms outstretched over his head. This is an example of a tight hamstring that is hampering the golf swing. Notice that Gina can't raise Lou's outstretched leg to 90 degrees.

HAMSTRING ROPE STRETCH

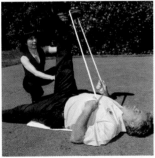

One easy way to stretch the hamstrings is to place a rope on the sole of the shoe. Lou keeps his back flat on the ground while holding the rope. He gently pulls his leg upward with the rope until he feels resistance, then holds that position for about 15 seconds while breathing normally. Slow is the key; stop when you feel increased resistance. Repeat several times. You may not be able to get the leg to 90 degrees even the first few times you do this exercise, but flexibility improvement will be noticeable. Stretching once a day is a good way to improve your flexibility in a controlled way.

STAND AND STRAIGHTEN EXERCISE

Gina coaches Lou to reach down and grab his toes while bending his knees.

Next, Lou keeps a slight bend in his knees, with his back flat, as he straightens his legs.

THE GOAL

After stretching his hamstring, Gina is able to raise Lou's leg to the 90-degree angle goal. Remember to do these drills for both legs to attain the level of flexibility that will help improve your game.

POWER IMPROVEMENT

Starting in the correct golf posture demonstrated earlier in this book, swing a medicine ball back and then release it along the target line represented by the golf shaft and ball.

LOWER BODY STRENGTH AND STABILITY IMPROVEMENT

Using a step training aid or something similar is an excellent way to create the needed stability you will need to whirl the club around your body. The pros on the PGA TOUR, Champions Tour and Nationwide Tour all have access to fitness trainers that stay with them for the duration of each tournament.

Body flexibility and the prevention of injuries enhance pros' abilities on the course. Pros take this phase of the game seriously, and they are in shape. Recreational golfers with a burning desire to improve need to follow the pros' example both on and off the course.

BASIC LOWER BODY LUNGE

Gina explains to Lou that he is incorrectly starting this exercise with his head looking down when it needs to be straight. Aside from that, here is the correct way to start the lunge. As the forward foot rests on the step, the knee is bent so the thigh is parallel to the ground. It is very important that the toe of the grounded foot points down and the heel is raised.

THE LUNGE

Lou stretches out while slightly lunging forward. It is very important not to let the forward knee go over the foot that is on the step. Repeat by changing leg positions.

ADVANCED LUNGE

This advanced exercise will improve the lower body strength, stability and upper body rotation. Lou lunges forward with a weighted ball. As he lunges forward, Lou keeps his abdominal muscles pulled inward.

Keeping his same lower body position, Lou rotates to the right with his upper body. Notice the head continues to look forward. The exercise will be repeated with Lou shifting leg positions and rotating to the left.

A Case for Stretching

Most recreational golfers hardly take the time to work on their games let alone their bodies. Because you are reading this book, you have a sincere desire to improve your game and have an open mind as to what it takes to accomplish this goal.

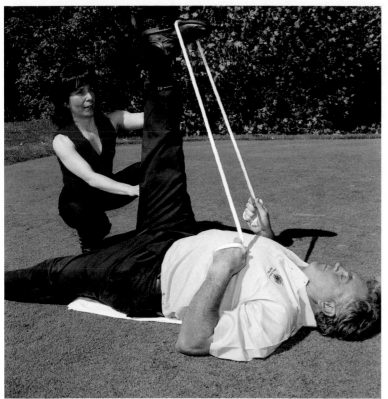

Incorporating a short stretching session into an everyday routine pays benefits both on and off the course. You will feel better, and it only takes a few minutes. PGA TOUR players leave nothing to chance. They fine-tune their equipment and bodies. Use them as positive role models.

Breaking Out
Work List for Success

1. Maintain a level of flexibility during the week so when you play your body is ready to score.

2. Never force or bounce yourself into a stretching position. Feel a slight muscle stretch and hold that position for about 15 seconds; repeat it two more times. You'll find your motion increases with each repetition.

3. Balance is vital to the golf swing. You are whirling a club around your body at speeds that, for some, will surpass 100mph. The body must be balanced to insure that the club impacts the ball on the sweet spot every time.

4. Do some of the stretches with your spouse or friend. Using this book as a visual guide, your partner can make sure you are in the correct positions.

5. Regularly do some self-tests to make sure your balance is correct.

Has Your
Body
Been
Holding
You Back?

157

INDEX

Index